Blackness
and Disability

Blackness and Disability

CRITICAL EXAMINATIONS AND CULTURAL INTERVENTIONS

EDITED BY
Christopher M. Bell

MICHIGAN STATE UNIVERSITY PRESS | *East Lansing* ■ LIT VERLAG | *Münster*

☉ The paper used in this publication meets the minimum requirements of ANSI/NISO Z39.48-1992 (R 1997) (Permanence of Paper).

LIT Verlag
Münster

 Michigan State University Press
East Lansing, Michigan 48823-5245

Printed and bound in the United States of America.

18 17 16 15 14 13 12 11   1 2 3 4 5 6 7 8 9 10

LIBRARY OF CONGRESS CATALOGING-IN-PUBLICATION DATA
Blackness and disability : critical examinations and cultural interventions / edited by Christopher M. Bell.
p. cm.
Includes bibliographical references.
ISBN 978-1-61186-010-8 (pbk. : alk. paper) 1. Minority people with disabilities—United States. 2. African Americans with disabilities. 3. People with disabilities—United States. I. Bell, Christopher M., d. 2009.
HV1569.3.M55B45 2012
305.9'0808996073—dc22
2011004494

Cover design by Sharp Des!gns, Inc.

g green Michigan State University Press is a member of the Green Press Initiative and is committed
press to developing and encouraging ecologically responsible publishing practices. For more
information about the Green Press Initiative and the use of recycled paper in book publishing, please visit
www.greenpressinitiative.org.

■ Visit Michigan State University Press at *www.msupress.msu.edu*

Contents

Sabine Broeck and Lennard Davis
Foreword and Acknowledgements   VII

Chris Bell
Introduction: Doing Representational Detective Work   1

Michelle Jarman
Coming Up from Underground: Uneasy Dialogues at the Intersections
of Race, Mental Illness, and Disability Studies   9

Cassandra Jackson
Visualizing Slavery: Photography and the Disabled Subject in the Art
of Carrie Mae Weems   31

Stella Bolaki
Challenging Invisibility, Making Connections: Illness, Survival, and
Black Struggles in Audre Lorde's Work   47

Therí Alyce Pickens
Pinning Down the Phantasmagorical: Discourse of Pain and the
Rupture of Post-Humanism in Evelyne Accad's *The Wounded Breast*
and Audre Lorde's *The Cancer Journals*   75

Robert McRuer
Submissive and Non-Compliant: The Paradox of Gary Fisher   95

Ned Mitchell
Sexual, Ethnic, Disabled, and National Identities in the "Borderlands"
of Latino/a America and African America   113

Chris Bell
"Could This Happen to You?": Stigma in Representations of the
Down Low   127

Moya Bailey
"The Illest": Disability as Metaphor in Hip Hop Music   141

Carlos Clarke Drazen
Both Sides of the Two-Sided Coin: Rehabilitation of Disabled
African American Soldiers   149

Notes on the Contributors   163

Foreword Sabine Broeck

How long have Black Studies managed to work with an epistemology of corpo-reality, bound to the materiality of oppression and abjection, how long has the field stressed, with acumen, the physicalness, as it were, of black endurance and resistance, without coming to address issues of 'disability'? This book fills a void that struck me as more than glaring when I sat in the 'blackness and disability'-workshop at the CAAR conference 2007 in Madrid. When I asked Christopher Bell, one of the motor forces behind this challenging workshop, if he could see himself collecting articles and editing a FORECAAST volume on this complex issue, he was immediately enthusiastic. In spite of the pains and obstacles of the protracted illness he himself struggled against with so much courage, stamina, and patience, Chris put together this collection of essays in the months after the Madrid conference. It pursues many of the pressing questions at the crossroads of 'blackness' and 'disability' in pioneering ways; without further ado, I can refer you to the introduction Chris himself had still managed to write. Hearing of Chris' passing in December 2009 plunged me into grief. The CAAR community lost an energetic member, radiant with intelligence and activism; I myself mourn the absence of a friend who delighted in everything from a good argument through the sight of a Vermont mountain range in the dusk, seen from the Burlington ferryboat, to fresh food, well cooked.

Before Chris passed away, he had sent a manuscript to me and the FORECAAST readers who had greeted its achievement. In January 2010, the FORECAAST board immediately agreed to publish the book in Chris' honor and memory. We are most grateful that Chris Bell's mother consented to publication in the FORECAAST series, as Chris had planned it originally. As the person who was entrusted by Chris' mother, his friends and colleagues with completing the present edition, I want to also extend my gratitude to all the collection's authors for their enduring faith in us that we'd manage to get it done despite many logistic delays, and to Chris' colleagues, Marcelle Haddix and Steven Taylor, who were most supportive in securing the final manuscript version and helping with other editorial matters. Thank you all!

Foreword Lennard Davis

About eight years ago, in a course I was teaching on disability studies, an African-American graduate student continually raised the issue that none of the readings concerned people of color. He also pointed out that not one of the major writers in the field was a person of color. And he continued to point out the essential "whiteness" of the field of disability studies. He had a point. For his final paper, he wrote a mock "Modest Proposal" along the lines of Swift's famous one. He proposed that we should just drop the pretense and openly proclaim that Disability Studies was "White Disability Studies."

The paper was arch, as any modest proposal should be, but it made sense, and made it in a performative way. I was impressed and asked him to expand the essay so I could include it in the second edition of *The Disability Studies Reader* which I was editing. That essay "modestly" attacked nothing short of all the major documents of disability studies, including my own book *Enforcing Normalcy*. It perhaps comes as little surprise, that the person I am describing is actually Christopher Bell, the editor of this new and most important work of disability studies.

Bell, and some other of my students, have concerned themselves deeply with the issue of race and disability, and a few of them are also contributors to this work. The good news, therefore, is that the sins of the teacher will not necessarily be visited upon the students. In fact, it is logical, reasonable, and just that one's students should pick up the work where one has left off. Indeed, there has been a gradual and now groundswell movement since the founding of disability studies to expand the insights of those early days to include the wide variety of identities included in the groups omitted in the intellectual census of race, gender, ethnicity, class, nationality, globality, queerness, and so on. New insights coming from these studies will expand and complicate our notions of disability.

It is perhaps ironic that I, who am a Jewish, male, straight, non-disabled, first-world academic should have been asked to write this foreword. The reality is that there are actually precious few full professors who teach disability studies. More are certainly in the academic pipeline. Senior scholars in this field, as Bell has noted, are almost exclusively white (although I do question that category when it is applied freely to groups that had been previously considered "of color" like Italians, Irish, Jews, Arabs, Turks, and others), and it is paradoxically a telling sign of the correctness of his argument that he has had to turn to me to write these words. In ten years from now, his turning to me will be seen as an act of desperation; now however it is an act of expedience.

The field of disability and race is a promising and necessary one, particularly because it will have to wrestle with shifting notions of identity and race. It had been a truism in academia that "there is no such thing as race" as a biological fact, while there is always of course racism. Yet recent developments in genomics have dramatically affected the first part of that truism. There may not be a biological proof for race, but increasingly it is becoming a new truth that there are "populations" with genetic signatures and these populations are related to geographical areas of origin. So one can comfortably say that a DNA test shows one to be part of the J1 haplotype, as my genetic group is called. I can confidently say that my male line is traceable back to people who came from what is now Northern Syria and that group contains many people of Jewish descent. With this kind of medicalization of identity, will race become a newly revived biological "fact" along with the medicalization of impairment?

With the advent of the first black president of the United States, does the concept of race change or will it change at all? We might want to contrast FDR with BHO – and we might want to think about the differences in considerations of race and disability over time. It's clear that FDR's race was invisible in the sense that whiteness is invisible and also at the same time very visible because only a white person could at that time have ruled the US. Roosevelt's mobility impairment was visible, but it was managed to make it seem as if the President could walk on his own (he never could). With the management of Roosevelt's impairment, he appeared to have mobility problems but not to be crippled. So he passed, in effect, for normal.

In the case of Roosevelt, the nation elected a mobility-impaired president, but ableism did not drop away from the American scene as a result. We can assume that racism will not wither away from the state now either. Yet in considering the intersectionality of race and disability how much does disability trump race? John McCain, Barack Obama's Republican adversary in the 2008 election, while white, did seem to have some disabilities resulting from his torture and poor medical care in Vietnam. His bodily conformation, limited motion of his arm, perhaps even physical tics, which were widely commented upon, and may have contributed to his lack of popularity – yet the same features could be thought of as "red badges of courage" resulting from his "heroism." Obama's race was discussed during the election as a possible issue interfering with voter enthusiasm (the Bradley effect), but at the same time his race never came into discussion as even remotely a disqualification for the job. (While McCain's post-traumatic syndrome was noted as an issue.) Can we see this election as proof that disability is the more discriminated against category when compared with race? We probably do not have enough information to make this a strong assertion. But this volume will help raise such questions. In exploring the gradients and variance of race joined with and opposed to disability, we can move toward understanding why it is that disability, along with race, remains such a hardy and persistent category of discrimination.

I wrote the previous paragraphs in February 2009. Ten months later Chris Bell had died during the complex dreariness of upstate New York winter darkness and the Christmas season. The loss of Chris was an enormous one for disability studies and for those of us who knew him personally. As I've indicated in the opening of this foreword, Chris was no shrinking violet and his loud, articulate, and often provocative voice had really been a spur and a goad to disability studies scholars to always think of race in the context of disability. His continuous and sometimes rankling imperative is one that we all need to provoke us, now in his permanent absence, to be ever mindful of the role of race, queerness, and chronic illness in the roil of identity and intersectionality in disability studies.

On a more personal note, I will miss Chris and his interventions. He was and always will be a memorable student. When he left the University of Illinois, he seemed to be perennially traveling from one speaking engagement to another, and always to the best places around the world. And he was perpetually on-line. I'll miss the continuous stream of articles and communications he forwarded. Most notably, he was the first person to inform me of the death of Edward Said, my dissertation director, colleague, and long-time friend. Chris remembered how important Said was, and as the first words appeared on the Internet, Chris fired them off to me with condolences. How sad now that I learned of Chris's death by a thoughtful e-mail letter from Steve Taylor, Chris's colleague at Syracuse University. As all were, I was shocked and devastated to learn about Chris's death. And like all around him, I wondered if I could have been more helpful to him. Chris had informed me when he was my student that he had problems with depression and other forms of emotional and physical distress with his struggle with AIDS. But it was easy to forget this side of Chris with his insouciant energy and his obvious delight in shaking up the status quo. In the end, his despair and demons got the best of him. But for me Chris will always be the man with the glint in his eye, a wry smile on his face, and what we might now call the "Bell imperative" to think more clearly, more politically, about disability. This book is a fitting tribute to that imperative.

Acknowledgements

Christopher Bell served as a Disability Studies Fellow at the Center on Human Policy, Law, and Disability Studies at Syracuse University from August, 2009, to December, 2010. Partial support for the editing of this volume and preparation of his introduction was provided by Grant # H133PO070014 awarded to the Center by the National Institute on Disability and Rehabilitation Research, U.S. Department of Education. The opinions expressed in this volume are those of the authors and do not necessarily reflect the position of the U.S. Department of Education.

Many people contributed directly or indirectly to the publication of this book. Marcelle Haddix and Steven Taylor of Syracuse University facilitated communications between the series editor and publisher and Christopher Bell's mother, Patricia A. Bell. The book has been published with the approval and full support of Ms. Bell. It is dedicated to her.

Sabine Broeck
November 2010

Chris Bell

Introduction: Doing Representational Detective Work

Diverging from the medical model of disability which argues that disabled subjects can and should be "fixed," Disability Studies views disability as socially-constructed much in the same way that other identities are. More specifically, Disability Studies scholars contend that cultural barriers preclude the full participation of disabled subjects in society similar to the ways that homophobia and heterosexism, racism, and sexism deter queer-identified, racial minority, and female subjects from operating at their fullest potential. The work of Disability Studies scholars has enlivened and richened discussions of corporeality and human diversity.

To reiterate, disability shares much in common with other maligned identities insofar as departures from the norm are seen as threats to the mainstream body politic. For instance, racial minorities are often characterized as inferior to white individuals. Such a misguided belief is a longstanding component of cultural attitudes towards disabled individuals as well. This is odd for several reasons, one of which bears particular underscoring: The politics of passing notwithstanding, it is unlikely that an individual will go to sleep one night and wake up a different race. Similarly, the process of changing biological sex is typically spread over months. Although some individuals alter their class status by winning the lottery or going bankrupt, the vast majority of individuals rarely experience drastic shifts in class. Not so with disability. Disability is, arguably, the only identity that one can acquire in the course of an instant.

We need look no further for evidence than Michele Wallace's classic feminist text *Black Macho and the Myth of the Superwoman*. In her description of Harriet Tubman, Wallace writes, "At the age of fifteen she intervened on behalf of another slave and was struck in the head by an overseer with a metal weight. *From then on* Harriet Tubman suffered dizzy spells and sleeping seizure" (151; my emphasis). Read one way, this description underscores the systematic violence overseers inflicted on slaves (a raced perspective). From another perspective, this description is premised on male domination of women (a gender perspective). A disability perspective (re)positions Tubman's instantaneous disabling alongside of her subsequent actions of attaining her own freedom and then returning to the South on numerous trips to liberate other slaves. Such daring action would be unremittingly dangerous for any individual; only if we factor in Tubman's bouts of illness, our understanding of her actions as well as her corporeality become fully accurate.

Tubman is certainly not the only historical figure whose disabled status is rarely spotlighted. In *Elegy for a Disease: A Personal and Cultural History of Polio*, Anne Finger summons Emmett Till, offering a reading of his life and death that may be surprising to some. I quote at length:

> the murder of Emmett Till in 1955 [was] one of the galvanizing events of the civil rights movement. Although Till's short life became legendary, few [know] that Till had been left with a speech impairment as a result of a bout with bulbar polio. His mother had taught him, when he had trouble speaking, to whistle in order to get his throat muscles to relax. Visiting relatives in Mississippi from his Chicago home, Till had been tortured and then murdered for having whistled at a white woman. His mother, Mamie Mobley, insisted on an open coffin for her son, wanting to make the brutality of Southern racism visible, and African American newspapers ran pictures on their front pages of his swollen and battered face. Until her death Mobley believed that the whistle leading to her son's death had been the result of an attempt to free his voice, rather than a wolf whistle directed at a white woman. (262)

Finger's assessment challenges us to reflect on the ways that Till's body was and is used for particular ends. Till is not the only victim of hate whose body has been used in these ways. Consider Disability Studies scholar Lennard Davis's reading of hate crime victim James Byrd, tied to a pick-up truck and dragged to death in Jasper, Texas in 1998:

> I recalled reading, on the day the crime was first reported, that a disabled African American had been brutally murdered. Since I was interested in disability, the article caught my eye. Yet when the story reappeared days, weeks, and months later, Byrd was simply referred to as African American. Almost all the news stories contained this simplification. Indeed, when I decided to write a piece on the subject for *The Nation*, I at first thought I might have made an error in thinking that Byrd was a person with disabilities. When I went to the library to look up the articles on microfilm, I found that the *New York Times* mentioned only twice, in the

first two reports, that Byrd was a person with disabilities. Any newspaper
story I checked tended to follow that pattern. (146)

It is not unusual to hear of a racially-motivated hate crime in the United
States of America. The fact that James Byrd has entered public consciousness
solely as a victim of such a crime is a disingenuous circumstance. The individuals targeting Byrd were undeniably "attracted" by his race. Yet it is important to
realize that Byrd was an individual who lived with severe arthritis. He had noti-
ceable difficulty walking down the street. Byrd, in the final analysis, was attacked because of race *and* disability. We do ourselves and his memory a disser-
vice in imagining and reporting otherwise.

Too much critical work in African American Studies posits the African
American body politic in an ableist (read non-disabled) fashion. Disability, as
we see in the examples of Tubman, Till, and Byrd, is relegated to the margins.
Similarly, as I argue in another forum, too much critical work in Disability Studies is concerned with white bodies: "Disability Studies, while not wholehear-
tedly excluding people of color from its critique, by and large focuses on white
individuals and is itself largely produced by a corps of white scholars and activists" (275). This volume is an intervention into the structuralist body politics underpinning African American studies and the whiteness at the heart of Disability
Studies.

I argue further that this collection is borne out of a desire to interrogate
the meanings and uses of "blackness" and "disability." Ned Mitchell's contribution is a prime example of this with its examination of an individual's rejection
of blackness and the implications of that rejection for the individual as well as
for those who come into contact with that individual. Mitchell's work is also
useful in the ways that it points the reader to the notion of disability in its ambiguity. AIDS is understood in his work as a disability. In contrast, in my contribution to the volume, which intentionally follows Mitchell's, I examine men on
the down low and never once refer to AIDS as a disability. I do so to call to
mind the shifting parameters of disability definition; the idea that some individuals with hidden disabilities are not "disabled enough."

The work of reading black and disabled bodies is not only recovery work,
as demonstrated in previously mentioned discussions of Tubman, Till, and Byrd,
but work that requires a willingness to deconstruct the systems that would keep
those bodies in separate spheres. This volume does the work of detection; it un-
covers the misrepresentations of black, disabled bodies and the missed oppor-

tunities to think about how those bodies transform(ed) systems and culture. This volume is an invitation to keep blackness and disability in conversation with one another. It is an invitation to rethink embodiment and representation.

This text is organized chronologically and thematically. Chronologically, the project begins with discussions of slavery and disability and concludes with an analysis of disability as a result of war, including the current one in Iraq. Thematically, the volume moves from studies of cognitive impairment and slavery in fiction to representations of slavery and violence in photography to deconstructions of illness (cancer and AIDS) narratives to comparative analyses of black and Latina/o and black and African subjects to analysis of treatments of disability in hip hop to, finally, commentary on disability, blackness, and war. These lines of demarcation are somewhat superficial if not entirely permeable. Since many of the contributors in this volume draw on key themes in Disability Studies and African American Studies, tactile connections are forged across genres and chronotopes.

Michelle Jarman's "Coming Up from Underground: Uneasy Dialogues at the Intersections of Race, Mental Illness, and Disability Studies" opens the collection by addressing the operations of mental health-related stigma in black communities in the US. She examines Campbell's final novel, illustrating how – in the novel and, arguably, in black culture – discourse about mental health remains out of favor. In her analysis, Jarman unpacks the complicated relationships in the novel, those related to mother/daughter dynamics, historical and contemporary understandings of "madness," as well as juridical-medical surveillance. Since Campbell's fictional text summons slavery, particularly the legacy of the Underground Railroad, Jarman's work is intentionally positioned prior to the next chapter which analyzes visual representations of the peculiar institution.

In "Visualizing Slavery: Photography and the Disabled Subject in the Art of Carrie Mae Weems," Cassandra Jackson offers a sustained critique of a well-known photograph of a slave referred to as "Gordon." By centering the work in the historical context of slavery, namely, through the lens of the physical violence inflicted on the body as well as the experience of trauma, Jackson queries the operations of memory as well as the effects and processes of what Marianne Hirsch has termed "postmemory."

The following two chapters, Stella Bolaki's "Challenging Invisibility, Making Connections: Illness, Survival, and Black Struggles in Audre Lorde's

Work" and Therí Pickens's "Pinning Down the Phantasmagorical: Discourse of Pain and the Rupture of Post-Humanism in Evelyne Accad's *The Wounded Breast* and Audre Lorde's *The Cancer Journals*," theorize concerns of physical violence and embodiment as related to cancer. As evident in the title of the chapters, Audre Lorde figures into both analyses although the approach is quite different.

Bolaki's work illuminates how Lorde worked to destabilize the performative modes that those receiving treatment for breast cancer were – and in many cases still are – expected to enact in concealing aspects of their experiences if not themselves. She traces Lorde's personal history of disability, focusing not just on her illness experiences and narratives, but on the other disabilities she lived with. In doing so, she demonstrates how Lorde lived the intersectionality she often wrote about.

Pickens's project takes a comparative approach, placing Lorde's discourse in conversation with that of another individual who received treatment for breast cancer, Evelyne Accad. In illustrating how both women negotiated the medical industrial complex by drawing on the support of a community of women, Pickens identifies the mechanisms of pain involved in breast cancer treatment as well as the potential for healing.

While Pickens is concerned with healing, the next contributor, Robert McRuer, is interested in rehabilitation, more specifically rehabilitation and its discontents. His contribution, "Submissive and Non-Compliant: The Paradox of Gary Fisher," discusses the cultural logic that led to Fisher referring to himself as a "black, queer sociopath." His work turns on AIDS, an illness that requires attentiveness not just to the lived experience of contagion but to the cultural experience of such. Fisher was largely if not unremittingly unapologetic about his subjectivity and its cultural dislocation. McRuer is intent on interrogating the reasons underpinning Fisher's dislocation, his absent presence.

Ned Mitchell's "Sexual, Ethnic, Disabled, and National Identities in the 'Borderlands' of Latino/a America and African America" is likewise concerned with absent presences, and the impact of AIDS, in queer of color communities. He considers the intersections of the titular identities in Piri Thomas's *Down These Mean Streets* and Susana Aiken and Carlos Aparicio's *The Transformation*. Mitchell's analysis is influenced by the theories of liminality put forth by Gloria Anzaldua, theories which encourage a reconsideration of cultural binaries, which insist that subjects choose between being one or another (or an "Other").

This thread of critiquing cultural binaries continues in "'Could This Happen to You?': Stigma in Representations of the Down Low." By examining the recent media frenzy surrounding men on the down low in US culture, Chris Bell calls into question performance-related aspects of masculinity that require black men to identify as straight or gay and the effects of that requirement. He is simultaneously concerned with cultural scapegoating as a result of fear of contagion.

Media analysis is at the heart of Moya Bailey's contribution, "'The Illest': Disability as Metaphor in Hip Hop Music." As she explains, a plethora of cultural work has been produced which examines misogyny, homophobia, and commercialism in hip hop. Absent from this discourse is a critique of ableism in the art form. In her meditation, Bailey reads hip hop lyrics in an effort at parsing the (mis)representation of disabled subjects within those lyrics.

The collection concludes with Carlos Clarke Drazen's "Both Sides of the Two-Sided Coin: Rehabilitation of Disabled African American Soldiers." In her work Drazen traces treatment approaches for disabled US veterans in the theaters of World War II and in the ongoing war in Iraq. She illuminates how attitudes towards rehabilitation in the first instance were predicated on attitudes towards the Civil Rights Movement and the black freedom struggle. Now, she suggests, treatment disparities are likely to be a result of entrenched racism as well as a misrecognition of what treatment specifically, and disability generally, signifies.

I close by acknowledging those who assisted in bringing this volume to fruition. First, I thank the contributors whose ideas and effort appears on the following pages. Thank you for trusting me with your work which I have learned a great deal from. My appreciation to the board of the Collegium for African American Research (CAAR) for supporting this volume in ways I am aware of as well as those I am not. For making the publication process seem practically seamless, *danke schön* to the staff of Lit Verlag. For providing office space of my own and a challenging intellectual community, thank you to the Center on Human Policy, Law, and Disability Studies at Syracuse University. Finally, I extend a nod of gratitude to CAAR President Sabine Broeck who could not have been any more selfless in the encouragement, insight and patience she extended to me. Thank you.

Works Cited

Bell, Chris. "Introducing White Disability Studies: A Modest Proposal." *The Disability Studies Reader*. 2nd ed. Ed. Lennard J. Davis. New York: Routledge, 2006. 275-82.

Davis, Lennard J. *Bending over Backwards: Disability, Dismodernism, and Other Difficult Positions*. New York: New York UP, 2002.

Finger, Anne. *Elegy for a Disease: A Personal and Cultural History of Polio*. New York: St. Martin's P, 2006.

Wallace, Michele. *Black Macho and the Myth of the Superwoman*. 1978. London: Verso, 1990.

Michelle Jarman

Coming Up from Underground: Uneasy Dialogues at the Intersections of Race, Mental Illness, and Disability Studies

As the field of disability studies has matured over the past few decades, especially in the United States, it has increasingly positioned itself as a minority discourse of social and cultural critique, pursuing unique, disability-specific analyses, but within a shared value system with race theory, gender/sexuality studies, and cultural area studies – especially in its commitment to challenge oppressive practices and pursue greater social justice. However, even with common values, building partnerships across disciplines has proven to be challenging. David Mitchell and Sharon Snyder suggest that one of the reasons the relationship between disability and multicultural studies has been "discomforting" is because as other minority fields have worked to liberate their identity categories "from debilitating physical and cognitive associations, they inevitably positioned disability as the 'real' limitation from which they must escape" (*Narrative Prosthesis* 2). Historically, this has been an important issue. The very real need to challenge fallacious biological attributes linked to race, gender, sexuality, and poverty – such as physical anomaly, psychological instability, or intellectual inferiority – has often left stigma around disability unchallenged – except by those specifically engaged in activism and in disability studies.

At the same time, in making claims for academic space and discursive legitimacy, disability studies scholars have often compared the extensive visibility of race and gender issues to the relative invisibility of disability perspectives. Lennard Davis, for example, argues that while race and ethnicity have become respected modalities from which to theorize and struggle politically over the last several decades, "disability has continued to be relegated to the hospital hallways, physical therapy tables, and the remedial classrooms" (xv). Mitchell and Snyder also stress the disparate academic fates between disability studies and other minority fields: "while literary and cultural studies have resurrected social identities such as gender, sexuality, class, and race from their attendant obscurity and neglect, disability has suffered a distinctly different disciplinary fate" ("Introduction" 1-2). While these arguments are valid and important, such comparisons have an unintended effect of putting these fields in unnecessary competition, as well as downplaying real differences and complicated intersections between gender, race, and disability. As Anna Mollow cogently points out, "if race and disability are conceived of as discrete categories to be compared, contrasted, or arranged in order of priority, it becomes impossible to think through complex intersections of racism and ableism in the lives of disabled people of color" (69). Following Mollow, I am distinctly interested in these connections, but at the same time, in looking beyond (multiple) identity categories, to the intricate ways discourses of race and disability have been linked historically, and continue to interweave.

This essay intends to consider some of the complex (dis)junctures between disability and race, specifically in relation to mental illness. My discussion is framed around Bebe Moore Campbell's final novel, *72-Hour Hold* (2005), a provocative narrative of an African American mother who struggles tenaciously to help her 18-year-old daughter, Trina, survive and manage the tumultuous, violent onset of bipolar disorder. Campbell's fictional yet realistic account highlights some of the ways mental distress – through social shame and stigma as well as medical ineffectiveness – is forced underground. The novel provides an interesting backdrop to discuss intersections and some of the difficult barriers between racial critiques and disability studies, but also invites an intersectional analysis and helps to point toward greater collaboration between them.

Bebe Moore Campbell, a best-selling African American author of numerous novels dealing with racial and social inequities, died unexpectedly in 2006, just a year after the publication of *72-Hour Hold*. Like much of her writing on divorce, childhood, racism, and interracial relationships, her portrayal of mental illness is rooted in personal experience. Campbell drew upon the experiences of a close family member who struggled with mental illness as a teenager and an adult to develop her representation of Trina (Fox, pars. 2-4). This novel is of particular interest because her portrayal of mental illness suggests many ruptures, gaps, and potential areas of discussion around historical and contemporary intersections of psychiatric treatment, disability, and race. While the novel actively exposes many failings of the psychiatric system, ultimately Campbell endorses medical understandings and treatments of mental illness. This stands in opposition to many psychiatric survivor approaches which largely reject "mental illness" as a coherent diagnostic category.

Also in potential conflict with disability studies scholarship, which has critiqued widespread and facile analogies between disability and disaster, trage-dy, and hopelessness, stands Campbell's extended metaphorical construct of mental illness as a form of slavery, and the positioning of her protagonist's quest to "liberate" her daughter from this psychiatric condition as a radical journey on a contemporary Underground Railroad. I contend that while this metaphor de-serves some critique, the imagery of a mother losing a daughter to slavery (ill-ness) also provides Campbell with a foundation to connect contemporary resis-tance and distrust of the dominant medical establishment to racialized histories of mental illness, and the very real dangers of being read as both "black" and "crazy" in the United States.

While *72-Hour Hold* provides a rich source of discussion, this essay also draws upon psychiatric survivor literature to push beyond the terrain of the nov-el. As many former psychiatric patients have detailed, the system itself is often far more abusive and violent than actual experiences of mental distress. Richard Ingram, for one, argues that in contrast to stereotyped notions of the "mad" as dangerous, those diagnosed with "mental illness" are, as he states, "less violent than the general population and positively docile in comparison with psychiatr-ists who practice 'involuntary commitment' and 'involuntary treatment' – also known as arbitrary incarceration, forced drugging, and electro-shock" (240).

Because there is much debate about the meaning and even existence of "mental illness," this essay makes a point of highlighting the contested nature of this term. In order to destabilize the dominant medical/psychiatric discourses around mental illness, which frame the experience in terms of "individual pa-thology" or "disorder," I often refer to mental distress, which attempts to chal-lenge the static nature illness diagnoses tend to impose. In addition, I refer to members of this group with terms that have emerged out of this movement, such as mental health service users, psychiatric system survivors, ex-users, and people with psychiatric disabilities. Anne Wilson and Peter Beresford rightly suggest that such language recognizes the self-determination of individuals who use or have used mental health services, but even more importantly, "disrupt[s] the perceived permanency of [diagnostic] labels" ("Genes" 543). While allowing that mental health services and traditional psychiatric diagnostic categories do fit the experiences of some people dealing with mental distress, these categories are often highly reductive, and imply a biological determinism that many survivors and ex-users resist.

Even as this essay challenges and expands upon some of the subject matter of the novel, I argue that Campbell's perspective and resolution, while pursuing an "overcoming" narrative that has been widely critiqued in disability studies, should be taken seriously. The author articulates an important critique of African American resistance to psychiatric diagnoses and mental health services. As well, her ultimate resolution of building support across broad identity lines and involving family (in its most complex, postmodern formation) to develop a powerful personal and political support system, is actually very much in line with African American and disability studies theoretical perspectives in their attempt to bridge material, discursive, and interpersonal divides.

The "Shackles" of Mental Illness?

As the title indicates, *72-Hour Hold* develops a telling critique of the current commitment standards and treatment practices for mental illness and distress. Following the journey of Keri and her daughter Trina, who has recently been diagnosed with bipolar disorder, Campbell focuses on the profound difficulties parents face in helping their young adult children through the onset of psychiatric disabilities. The novel centers around a period shortly after Trina turns eighteen, and has stabilized on a medication regimen. Suddenly, however, Trina begins smoking marijuana, stops taking her meds, and begins a cycle of manic and depressive behaviors. As Campbell captures, rather than building greater awareness about and acceptance of psychiatric difference, the public venue for mental illness remains a theater for the spectacle of "madness" – and without psychiatric intervention, the risks (especially to a young African American woman) of being hurt, exploited, or going to jail, increase exponentially. Although forced hospitalization is a horrible "choice" for Keri, because there are so few options for better support for people in the midst of mental distress, this often becomes the only and best hope for intervening in her daughter's self-destructive cycles.

By positioning Keri as the narrative voice of the novel, readers discover and interpret Trina's experience of bipolar disorder through her mother. In fact, the novel is more about Keri coming to terms with the diagnosis than it is about Trina's experience, which will be discussed at more length. In order to convey the intensity of Keri's shock and pain, Campbell develops an extended metaphor of mental illness as slavery; Keri's experience of "losing" Trina to her illness becomes a vivid and horrific reenactment of ancestral black mothers losing their children on auction blocks. Within this imagery, Keri is positioned as a figure reminiscent of Harriet Tubman in her determined quest to liberate her daughter from the "shackles" of her illness.

Early in the novel, Keri describes her reaction to Trina's illness in terms of chattel slavery:

> I could feel her breath on my face, see the flames rioting in her eyes. That's when I knew she wanted to hurt me. I knew that what was wrong was soul deep and strong as chains. [...] *My baby is sick.* [...] I embarked on the Middle Passage that night, marching backward, ankles shackled. I journeyed to a Charleston auction block, screaming as my child was torn from my arms, as I watched her being driven away. Trina didn't belong to me anymore. Something more powerful possessed her. (29)

On the surface, the conflation of Trina's manic behavior with enslavement suggests a blanket rejection of disability and illness in troubling and all too familiar terms – as a hostile invasion, a sudden threat to autonomy, independence, and future dreams. This metaphor is highly problematic as a representation of Trina's experience because it ties everything about Trina to her diagnosis – to a static idea of (people with) mental illness as dangerous, unpredictable, irrational, and wholly without insight. Slavery, which derives its very power from a cruel history of oppression and brutality, connects only extremely negative connotations to the experience of mental illness. In effect, the metaphor reduces mental illness to a dehumanized life. In many ways, the imagery of the auction block forecloses more generative ideas around psychiatric disabilities and accepts limited, socially imposed regulations about appropriate cognitive processes. Andrea Nicki, whose work focuses on feminist theory and psychiatric disability, points out that we are culturally trained to see specific kinds of behaviors as non-normative, even when they could be advantageous. She talks about mania in particular, as a form of thought that is not appreciated: "It is a world where abilities heightened in mania – fluency of thought, verbal fluency, or the ability to rapidly produce relevant, original, or innovative ideas – do not cause appreciation or admiration in others but, rather, distress, fear, or anger" (90). This belief system is imbedded within Campbell's imagery, where Trina's illness seems to be pulling her irretrievably into an abyss.

However, while the conflation of mental illness and slavery is deeply problematic, the imagery does provide an evocative narrative structure for Keri's struggle with her daughter's radically unpredictable behavior. Importantly, on a historical level, Campbell's evocation of slavery calls forth the particular legacies of white on black racism in the U.S. as constitutive of understanding the social and cultural constructions of mental illness. From a contemporary perspective, this reference mirrors the blatant failures of the medical and psychological establishments in serving people with psychiatric diagnoses. In addition, by haunting a twenty-first century, ostensibly realistic account of mental illness with slavery and the quest for liberation, readers are pushed to consider how forms of oppression, be they social, racial, medical, or physical, continually collide – often with rather messy results.

As the quote above demonstrates, Campbell's decision to narrate the novel from the mother's perspective provides an externalized perspective of disability, but offers a lens into Keri's parental (and political) choice to fight for (and sometimes against) Trina in order to protect her from the dangers of her own behavior as well as from the psychiatric system set up to treat her. In that moment of recognizing that Trina is *really* mentally ill – not on drugs, stressed out, or rebelling – she realizes she can't control or predict what will happen to her daughter. When Trina walks out into the night, her mind racing in her private mania, communicated in part by her provocative attire – a "micromini red leather skirt," her mouth "a slash of iridescent white" (24) – and by her determination to fight her way out the door, she is "*gonegonegonegonegone...*" to her mother in a way that transcends ordinary teenage rebellion. The mantra ringing in Keri's mind "*gonegonegone...*" evokes the auction block, and places her fight for Trina's mental balance into a historical struggle to protect the coherence of the African American family against external and internal threats.

In his classic study, *Slavery and Social Death*, Orlando Patterson terms this process of familial destruction "natal alienation" (7), stressing that it was a crucial element of slavery. In order for slave owners to transform free human beings into enslaved captives, all ties to family and heritage had to be excised:

> Not only was the slave denied all claims on, and obligations to, his parents and living blood relations but, by extension, all such claims and obligations on his more remote ancestors and on his descendants. He was truly a genealogical isolate. [...] Slaves differed from other human beings in that they were not allowed freely to integrate the experience of their ancestors into their lives [...] or to anchor the living present in any conscious community of memory. (5)

Within the novel, not only does Keri respond to the all too real history of African American mothers having their children stolen through institutionalized slavery, but she also confronts the potential loss of familial and ancestral memory that Trina's illness seems to threaten.

Prior to the onset of bipolar disorder, Trina had been an exceptional, devoted student who earned early acceptance to Brown University. Since Keri's divorce from Trina's father, Clyde, when Trina was very young, mother and daughter have lived together and forged a formidable, intimate bond with one another, the memory of which seems to fade for Trina when in the midst of a manic or depressive cycle. It is this loss of connection – of family cohesion – that most disturbs Keri. In the most extreme moments, Trina becomes violent and aggressive, at one point breaking every window in the house before leaving in a fury. Further severing their familial bond, the most common "delusional" accusation Trina makes is that Keri is not her real mother – that she is a demon trying to kill her. On one level, Trina knows this is the most cruel thing she can say to her mother, and it certainly elicits the most pervasive fear in Keri – that indeed her daughter (and perhaps Keri herself) might become a "genealogical isolate," an individual whose most important familial bonds will be irretrievably lost.

While Trina ultimately is well served by psychiatric treatment, Keri's feelings of powerlessness and despair notably grow out of her intense desire to restore Trina to her pre-diagnostic state. The "shackles" Campbell depicts are fastened to Keri's ankles, not Trina's, and Keri's attachment to what she had imagined as her daughter's perfect future causes her most intense feelings of loss. Although Keri accepts Trina's diagnosis, she remains unwilling to envision a different future for Trina than the one her beautiful, smart daughter had been carving out before the onset of mental distress. Throughout much of the novel, Keri resists any suggestion that Trina will not make what she considers a full recovery – in other words, that she will return to Brown University, and continue to excel academically, open new doors of opportunity, and flourish socially.

As the novel progresses, however, Campbell makes clear that Keri's attachment to this particular future functions as a perceptual bind that must be released. This is not to say that Keri shouldn't continue to hope for and believe in a wonderful future for her daughter, but to stress that the only way she seems to be able to imagine a positive future is through removing Trina's mania and depression. Memory, in this sense, functions both to strengthen Keri's resolve to help her daughter, and to limit her ability to imagine the multiple potentialities of Trina's future *with* a psychiatric diagnosis. Keri's struggle, however, reflects a problematic binary set up by psychiatric discourse itself, which pushes patients to come to terms with their diagnoses, and accept prognoses of greatly limited futures. In their experiences with psychiatric professionals, both Anne Wilson and Peter Beresford stress that they were encouraged to acknowledge the truth of their "illness" diagnoses, and an essential part of that process was to accept diminished (not just different) dreams for their futures. They were told they might be able to work at low levels, but not to expect too much: "With the benefit of hindsight, it seems to us now that the psychiatrists' 'prognoses' were concerned with devaluing and subverting our understanding of ourselves" ("Madness" 153).

Traditional psychiatric models classify people as either ill or not ill, and accepting illness diagnoses demands that compliant patients accept new, limited, and diminished understandings of themselves. From this perspective, Keri's refusal to let go of her dreams for Trina is partly an act of resistance, but the binary reflected in the contrast between Trina as ill/doomed to failure versus Trina as well/destined for success, is very much constructed by the medical model of mental illness as a static, lifelong condition that will greatly limit one's ability to achieve. In order to expand her ideas about Trina's potential futures, Keri has to deconstruct this binary that boxes her daughter into a predetermined future, and hinders her from believing in Trina's potentially exciting, unknown future. As Keri's journey reflects, limiting people's futures can be far more oppressive than the illness itself.

Campbell positions her critique of the psychiatric system within a historical structure in which cultural meanings of race and madness have been intricately entwined. By framing her narrative of modern mental illness within the memory of slavery and the arduous drive for liberation represented by the Underground Railroad, Campbell reminds readers of the long history of racist misappropriations of "madness," not only to justify social oppression, but to perpetuate the so-called rationality of slavery itself. For example, so convinced were many slave owners of the "natural hierarchies" of the races, they believed anyone attempting to escape bondage was exhibiting tell-tale signs of "mental illness." Medical doctors agreed, and offered up detailed sketches of such disorders in complicated language in order to solidify the medical "truth" of racially specific aberrations of the mind. In 1851, Dr. Samuel Cartwright provided the following descriptions of psychopathologies to which African Americans alone were prey in the *New Orleans Medical and Surgical Journal*: "drapetomania" referred to "the diseases causing slaves to run away," but an even more common diagnosis, one running rampant among plantation slaves was "dysaesthesia aethiopis or hebetude of mind" – the scientific and formal medical term for what overseers more casually called "rascality." Clarifying this medical diagnosis (in political terms), Cartwright detailed the meaning of this mental condition: "According to unalterable physiological laws, negroes, as a general rule [...] can only have their intellectual faculties in a sufficient degree to receive moral culture, and to profit by religious or other instruction, when under the compulsory authority of the white man" (698). Racial, biological, and political authority were united under this theory to naturalize the continued oppression of African Americans, an oppression deeply tied to deterministic medical constructions of moral and mental (in)capacities.

Even more egregious was the idea that freedom from slavery actually caused mental illness. Sander Gilman traces how this argument was put forth in the U.S. in 1840 using the newly (and shockingly inaccurate) census data. According to their results, of the 17,000 cognitively impaired people across the nation, 3,000 of them were African American. As Gilman states, "If these staggering census statistics were to be believed, free blacks had an incidence of mental illness eleven times higher than slaves and six times higher than the white population" (137). Although the census turned out to be based upon flagrantly false data (such as a listing of 133 black insane paupers in Worcester, MA – a town with a total population of 151), this didn't hinder anti-abolitionists from using census numbers to argue that slavery actually kept African Americans sane.

Such spurious arguments, of course, continued well after emancipation. In the International Medical Congress of 1887, J. B. Andrews claimed shocking increases of insanity and mental illness among the black population between 1870 and 1880, which he attributed directly to liberation from slavery: "The causes are briefly told: enlarged freedom, too often ending in license; excessive use of stimulants; excitement of the emotions, already unduly developed; the unaccustomed strife for means of subsistence: educational strain and poverty" (qtd. in Rosen 190). By the early twentieth century, eugenics continued this partnership between medical and scientific discourse to promote baseless connections between blackness and cognitive inferiority. Although many leading eugenicists focused upon the improvement of the white race, they were eager to use mental testing and family histories to "objectively" demonstrate the lower mental capacity of targeted groups, especially poor, uneducated whites, growing immigrant groups, and African Americans.

These diagnostic practices could be dismissed into historical obscurity if scientific racism didn't continue to target African Americans, and attempt to reduce social and economic issues to biomedical "pathologies." Vanessa Jackson, who has attempted to reconstruct some of the lost histories of African Americans with psychiatric diagnoses, points out that in the late 1960s, a prominent study suggested that "urban violence, which most African Americans perceived as a reaction to oppression, poverty, and state-sponsored economic and physical violence against us, was actually due to 'brain dysfunction,' and recommended psychosurgery to prevent outbreaks of violence" (5). Not only were these studies taken seriously, but references to "brain dysfunction" in federally funded initiatives against violence continued to surface well into the 1990s.

Bridging Race and Disability Critiques
These examples, while only touching the surface of the various ways scientific and medical research have participated in racialized, oppressive practices, gesture toward the power of disability designations – especially psychiatric diagnoses – to discredit individuals and groups. Historian Douglas Baynton has documented how attributes of physical and mental disability were used against immigrants, African Americans, and women in early twentieth-century citizenship debates. As he explains, "not only has it been considered justifiable to treat disabled people unequally, but the concept of disability has been used to justify discrimination against other groups by attributing disability to them" (33). The most common methods of resisting such strategies of social disqualification, Baynton goes on to point out, has been to claim soundness of mind and physical competence – rather than to disavow prejudice based upon medicalized designations. In other words, while racialized biomedical or psychiatric diagnoses are rightly rejected and exposed, arguments resisting misapplied diagnoses writ large – in this case those of "brain dysfunction" and "mental illness" – often have the effect of solidifying the stigma already attached to disability. This passage from Baynton is useful in elucidating this dilemma:

> This common strategy for attaining equal rights, which seeks to distance one's own group from imputations of disability and therefore tacitly accepts the idea that disability is a legitimate reason for inequality, is per-

haps one of the factors responsible for making discrimination against people with disabilities so persistent and the struggle for disability rights so difficult. (51)

With the long history of those benefiting by a power structure based upon white privilege using medical and psychiatric diagnoses to manufacture "truths" of racial inferiorities, vehement resistance to such reasoning has been essential. However, a longstanding disconnection between the critiques of racial and disability prejudice tends to reinforce the idea that medical designations, unless false, are individual "problems," not social or political issues in need of analysis. Deborah Marks suggests a useful way to consider the interaction of disability and race as processes of constructing otherness. Drawing from Stuart Hall, she argues that his most cited questions addressed to seeming outsiders – "Why are you here?" and "When are you going to go home?" – are analogous to questions constantly addressed to disabled people, which she frames as, "How did you get like that?" and "Can you be cured?" (47). While Hall frames these questions to migrants, they are worth considering as underlying mechanisms at work in perpetuating ideas of racial separateness and distance. Marks' related questions, in their insistence upon explaining and erasing difference, provide a productive way of thinking about racism and ableism as intersecting processes of exclusion. As Marks explains further, "Both [sets of] questions interpolate an 'outsider,' someone not like me, whose existence presents a problem to me" (47). This layered interplay of racial and disability stigma informs contemporary responses to mental distress, and, as Campbell represents in her novel, compounds and complicates the struggles experienced by African Americans with psychiatric diagnoses.

By gesturing toward slavery and the (mis)associations between mental illness and blackness, Campbell traces out the several important contemporary issues among African Americans connected to this history. First, while Campbell clearly critiques the legacies of specious racialized misappropriations of science, she also suggests that the resistance to this racist history within some African American communities has been an outright denial of psychiatric disability, which often poses serious problems to people who could benefit from mental health support services. Second, in tracing out a story of an underground network of alternative support, Campbell develops a sustained critique of the psychiatric system and the limited choices available to people in mental distress and their allies.

Campbell portrays the common cultural resistance to mental illness and psychiatric intervention through Trina's parents' conflicting interpretations of her behavior and needs. Keri, who lives with Trina and bears witness to her daughter's extreme mental and emotional changes, comes to accept Trina's diagnosis of bipolar disorder, and seeks out medical and emotional support for both of them. Trina's father, Clyde, who sees his daughter only occasionally, insists that her erratic behavior stems from ordinary stresses. Further, Clyde implies that Keri is overreacting and only making Trina worse by forcing her into therapy. He insists that Trina would be "better off without some shrink putting ideas into her mind" (69). Even when Trina is put on a 72-hour hold for hitting someone in her therapy group, Clyde is incensed, and wants Trina released: "So what if she hit someone? Maybe the person deserved it. Maybe he did something to her. I'm getting her out of here" (92). Keri, who has been living with Trina and watching her slip into manic behaviors – smoking marijuana, refusing to take her medication, acting increasingly aggressive – agrees with the involuntary hold, and hopes it will get Trina back on her medication. Clyde's desire to protect Trina from being held against her will is understandable, but Campbell makes clear that his resistance to the hold comes from an ongoing denial of the seriousness of Trina's distress. His unwillingness to see all aspects of the situation makes him ill-equipped to help his daughter, and unable to consider Keri's viewpoint. Watching Clyde pace in the hospital halls, Keri realizes she has to rely on herself: "In theory, we should have gone to plan Trina's aftercare together, but it was clear we weren't playing on the same team" (93).

In her interviews with several African Americans diagnosed with mental illness, Vanessa Jackson describes such resistance as that depicted by Campbell as commonplace: "Even in extremely supportive families there was a willingness to talk about anything but the mental illness. Families were able to have weekly visits or phone calls to loved ones in the hospital yet still not acknowledge the mental illness" (17). Within the novel, Campbell suggests this denial extends beyond families to African American communities more broadly. This is portrayed in Keri's "trek" out of her neighborhood to seek support for Trina and for herself. As she describes, she travels a good distance from Crenshaw, a largely black community in South Central Los Angeles, to the west side, the "land of high real estate, fair-skinned people, and the coldest ice":

Part of me resented having to trek all the way from Crenshaw to get help for my child's issues. But the truth was, mental illness had a low priority on my side of the city, along with the color caste and the spread of HIV. Some things we just didn't talk about, even though they were killing us. So I had to come to the white people, who, although just as traumatized, were a lot less stigmatized by whatever went wrong in their communities. (49)

Within this group, Keri quickly bonds with three other African American parents who have children in mental distress. Milton and Gloria, who are married, and Mattie, all become her new support group. Upon meeting the first time, they joke about being "the only black people in America willing to admit having mental illness in our families." As Keri says, "[B]eing black is hard enough. Please don't add crazy" (50).

As Campbell goes public with the issue of mental illness within black communities, she firmly resists the legacy of white feminist representations of the "madwoman" as a figure of rebellion or empowerment. Campbell's depiction of Trina follows Shoshana Felman's assertion that "quite the opposite of rebellion, madness is the impasse confronting those whom cultural conditioning has deprived of the very means of protest or self-affirmation" (8). As Campbell argues, this is especially true for black people, who are also in particular danger of being arrested, treated violently, and even shot if they are seen in public acting "crazy." She weaves the story of "Crazy Man," a mentally distressed homeless man who has become a fixture in Crenshaw, as a way of illustrating the potentially fatal consequences of public displays of "madness." During the period when Trina stops taking her medication and becomes increasingly unpredictable, Keri hears that "Crazy Man" has been gunned down in the street by police. According to people Keri talks to in the neighborhood, he had been running down the street, screaming that the CIA was after him, and tearing his clothes off. As Keri's friend concludes from the incident, "When somebody black get to acting a fool out in these here streets, the cops gonna shoot'em and go on about they business" (137).

Naturally, Keri's immediate reaction is fear for Trina: "It could have been Trina. [...] My child could have been the one being buried. She could have walked out of my house, bent on mayhem and destruction. There wasn't anything I could do to protect her" (137). The reality that public displays of mental illness can be dangerous, even fatal – especially to non-white people – drives Keri to participate in a radical underground psychiatric intervention for her daughter. Frustrated by the standards required to put Trina on a 72-hour hold, especially now that she is over eighteen, and feeling increasingly isolated and desperate to effect some kind of stability, Keri joins a clandestine group of psychologists, parents, and other mental health providers who work outside the bounds of the law in order to provide what they consider to be better, more holistic treatment. The leader of the group, Brad, likens their work to the Underground Railroad: "Mental illness is a kind of slavery. Our movement is about freeing people too," he explains to Keri. "We won't always have to hide and run to do our work in the dark. The day is coming when people with brain diseases won't be written off or warehoused, when everyone will know recovery is possible" (175).

Keri and her friend Bethany, who introduces her to Brad and his group, decide to put their daughters into the program together. Worried about Trina's stability, they take her directly from the hospital after a hold. In order to get Trina to come with them, Keri lies and tells her a friend is giving them a ride home. Once in the car, however, as Trina realizes she's being taken against her will, she (reasonably) becomes angry and volatile, and as Keri explains where they're all going, Brad sedates Trina with Haldol, which makes both mother and daughter angry. Soon Keri realizes she has given up control to these people, and begins to wonder if she's made the right choice. As they travel, they meet with different psychologists who get Trina and Angelica, Bethany's daughter, stabilized on medications. They move from safe house to safe house, which are mostly homes of other parents whose children have been in the program. Keri gains perspective from their stories, and Trina, even as she becomes more calm emotionally, remains defiant about being under the control of strangers: "Why can't we just go home?" she asks Keri repeatedly, and when her pleas are ignored she complains, "These people are devils" (219). Keri hears Trina, but hopes that as she continues to stabilize on her medication, she will understand.

As they continue, the people involved in this psychiatric underground demonstrate their commitment and competence, even as they hit snags in the road. One of the most interesting aspects of the approach, which relies on a combination of medication, work, exercise, and structured entertainment, is the full involvement of everyone, including Keri and Bethany. Upon deciding to join Brad's group, both mothers also commit to traveling with them for at least a month. Angelica, Trina, Keri, Bethany, and Brad, sleep on cots in a locked room, so even though the two daughters are being held against their wills, they are always with Keri, Bethany, and others in the group. During this period, the analogy between their psychiatric program and the Underground Railroad come into sharp relief as everyone involved realizes the risks they have taken. While staying in one safe house, Trina escapes long enough to wave down a car and yell for the driver to save her. Although the car doesn't stop, a few days later, the police show up, and the whole group has to move quickly. Keri doesn't like being out of the driver's seat, but in making this journey, she has chosen to tie herself to Trina and her psychiatric disability in a much deeper way. She isn't simply supportive; she's walking on the path with Trina. Thinking back to Tubman, Keri wonders to herself, "What would Harriet do with this? No time to plan. Nowhere to run. But the same imperative, the same need to cross the border. To save herself. To save another" (119).

Notably, "saving herself" becomes essential to the process, and the underground journey does cause Keri to change. Initially, she insists upon making comparisons between Trina and Angelica, whom she considers to be much sicker than her daughter, but gradually she realizes that these comparisons are useless and hurtful. In fact, the comparison game just provides a structure for excluding all people with mental illness, some more than others. As they learn more about each other, and fight battles together, Bethany and Keri move beyond the separations of white/black, of bipolar/borderline to being warriors together, sisters in their determination to be there for their daughters, whatever that means. Also, as she lives with more and more people and listens to their stories, she begins to let go of her defiant attachment to Trina's intellectual brilliance, and allow the future to be a real unknown. Although it is beyond the scope of Campbell's novel to suggest widespread systemic solutions, in tracing out a modern resistance to the ineffectual support offered to Trina, the author attempts to move the conversation beyond racial disparities and psychiatric stigma into one of collaborative support and dialogue among professionals, mental health users, and their allies.

Ultimately, however, this underground alternative doesn't provide the perfect panacea for Keri or Trina. At the first opportunity, Trina escapes one of the safe houses, and ends up back in the hospital. After this, Keri turns back to legal channels, gains conservatorship, and – with the help of Trina's father – has her daughter committed, which, in this fictionalized account, finally brings her back into mental "balance." This resolution, while remaining critical of an imperfect system, endorses the idea that coercion, confinement, and control are sometimes crucial to the healing process, and that the well meaning parents or loved ones need even greater power over those struggling with mental distress. I don't dispute the tenor of Campbell's narrative of Keri, implying that decisions to incarcerate and restrict one's child or loved one comes as a last resort. However, the great irony of the novel is that the author's driving analogy of slavery, while successfully highlighting the fraught historical intersections of madness and blackness, too easily conflates illness with oppression, rather than challenging the myriad and complex ways psychiatric, medical, and social responses to mental illness enact forms of bondage often far more traumatic for those struggling with periods of distress.

Challenging Isolation, Listening to Distress, and Building Alliances

By focusing the narrative on treating and managing Trina's diagnosis, Campbell misses an opportunity to look at the ways her enslavement analogy might be applied to the medical and social oppression and disenfranchisement experienced by those considered mentally ill. In addition, because Keri is the central figure in this struggle (instead of Trina), the structure of the novel mirrors the cultural tendency to read people experiencing mental distress purely from a diagnostic perspective, and to silence their unique interpretations of their experience. Keri's initial reaction to Trina's diagnosis is telling in this respect. When the doctor says Trina is bipolar, Keri is incensed – and resistant: "That was the scariest part, the way he said it. She *is* bipolar, not she *has* bipolar *disorder*. You *are* cancer. You *are* AIDS. Nobody ever said that" (25). Keri doesn't want to see her daughter this way, but in many ways this becomes her central struggle. For much of the novel, she seems to bend to this understanding, in the sense that the illness becomes the *enslaver* – the enemy Keri feels she has to defeat to liberate her daughter. This intense medicalization, however, also drives the novel to challenge and question these reductive impulses. Campbell rehashes these limitations, but also poses crucial questions: How does one accept a psychiatric diagnosis, seek treatment, but also challenge the stigma associated with mental illness? How should the system change to allow for the need to occasionally protect people in mental distress through involuntary holds while remaining equally committed to respecting and protecting their personhood?

Some of the reductiveness inherent in psychiatric models are animated by Campbell's representation of Trina, both in what is included and what is absent. For much of the novel, Trina is figured largely as an embodiment of bipolar disorder. Although readers see Trina's perspective somewhat, her complaints and comments during manic or depressive periods are used to demonstrate distress or delusion, rather than to offer forms of knowledge. Catherine Prendergast argues that the constructions of psychiatric diagnoses function to "rhetorically disable" those who find themselves so labeled. In her field of rhetoric, Prendergast suggests that this might be more aptly understood as "a life denied signification" (57). This denial of personhood is enacted by the psychiatric profession's insistence that mental health clients have "no insight," which from a clinical perspective, means they refuse to accept their illness diagnoses. In other words, as Prendergast stresses, once diagnosed, patients (as they are now defined) are not able to produce their own narrative of their experience, especially if this differs from medically imposed interpretations (53). Christopher Canning, an advocate of integrating psychiatric survivor testimonials into any kind of treatment program, echoes Prendergast's concerns. He points out that very little attention is given to the ways people in mental distress understand their own world, because of a longstanding belief that an ill mind cannot, by definition, know itself (par. 10). The result of dismissing the words, feelings, and testimonies of people in states of mental distress is ultimately to rob them of personal signification, and to force their understanding of their own lives into an involuntary hold of its own.

In a similar vein, psychiatric system survivors Anne Wilson and Peter Beresford argue that the monolithic nature of the dominant discourse surrounding mental illness "accentuat[es] and perpetuat[es] [...] distress and 'difference' through the construction of users of mental health services as Other – a separate and distinct group" (144). This othering invokes a false binary, and continually pushes mentally distressed individuals outside the fold of personal autonomy and social participation. These authors admit that although they have both experienced mild and extreme mental distress, an approach that would integrate a social and medical model would see these experiences along a continuum, not as fixed or static expressions of psychosis or neurosis: "we place ourselves alongside everyone else on a continuum of mental and emotional distress and well-being: a continuum that does not show binary opposition between 'the mad' and 'the not-mad'" (154).

Ultimately, Campbell provides more room for Trina's perspective to emerge, and gestures toward this continuum. When she finally returns home after her extended hospital stay, Trina begins to talk about her illness with her grandmother, whose history with alcoholism provides her with unique insight and compassion. This conversation between Trina and Emma points toward the idea that mental illness dwells within a broad continuum of human variation, not as something wholly other:

> "How are you getting on?" [Emma] asked.
> "I'm doing better, Grandma," Trina said.
> "Sometimes it takes a while to get better. I was sick for a long time. [...] I'm an alcoholic, Trina. When I go out in the evenings, I'm going to my AA meetings. They keep me from drinking."
> "I go to meetings too."
> "I know."
> "What do you do at your meetings?"
> "Talk, mostly."
> "Mine too. But you don't take medicine."
> "Not for being an alcoholic. I take high-blood-pressure medicine. If I don't, I'll get sick."
> "If I don't take my medication, I'll get sick. There's something wrong with my brain."
> Emma laughed. "Mine too." (317)

In many ways, Trina's journey to understanding and proactively addressing her mental distress and health is in its beginning stages at the close of the novel, and her anger (and appreciation) over being hospitalized promise to inform her ongoing knowledge of living with her diagnosis. Her grandmother's presence also provides a sense of process, not of cure or completion. She reminds Trina that medication, meetings, and recovery may be a part of her life for a long time, and that these pieces are hers to situate and infuse with meaning.

Conclusion

Campbell's decision to narrate the novel from Keri's perspective, however, allows her to explore and value the unique struggles faced by family members and allies of those in mental distress. As Trina adjusts to experiencing manic and depressive states, Keri also has to face extreme changes in her daughter's manner and behavior. As she witnesses Trina's increasingly self-destructive tendencies, she decides the only way to help her is to forcibly get her back on medication. Any parent, family member, or ally who has felt compelled to make such a contradictory decision on behalf of someone in a state of distress understands the unyielding guilt, self-doubt, and pain involved. In taking on mental illness as the driving force of her novel, Campbell encourages a more public acceptance and dialogue of all forms of mental distress, so that the struggles people face will no longer be compounded by cultural stigma. As well, the novel suggests that as better treatments are imagined – treatments which don't require parents and allies to break the law and retreat to underground collectives – an active dialogue between those diagnosed with mental illness and their families or chosen allies should inform new models as well. The perspectives of allies should never be used to silence the voices of psychiatric system survivors or mental health users, but Campbell's point that parents and allies are all deeply invested in and insightful about developing better mechanisms of support and treatment should be taken seriously.

Campbell's endorsement of psychiatric intervention might be seen as opposing the important insights of system survivors, but I would suggest that these perspectives should inform and complement each other. I agree with Elizabeth Donaldson, who argues that "it is possible [...] to begin with the premise that mental illness is a neurobiological disorder and still remain committed to a [...] disability studies agenda – an agenda that fights discriminations [and] seeks to dismantle ideologies of oppression" (112). In an effort to respect the voices of all people with psychiatric disabilities, challenging the stigma of mental illness must include guarding against monolithic discourses, and instead push toward expanding our ideas about and acceptance of cognitive diversity. The most inspiring notions tying the Underground Railroad to mental illness is that people without psychiatric diagnoses choose to link their fates to those with psychiatric diagnoses, in the ultimate sense of risking themselves (and ourselves) to the treatments designed for others. Perhaps in this deep connection, those without diagnoses will see more clearly what is at stake.

Works Cited

Baynton, Douglas. "Disability and the Justification of Inequality in American History." *The New Disability History: American Perspectives*. Ed. Paul K. Longmore and Lauri Umansky. New York: New York UP, 2001. 33-57.

Beresford, Peter, and Anne Wilson. "Genes Spell Danger: Mental Health Service Users/Survivors, Bioethics and Control." *Disability & Society* 17.5 (2002): 541-53.

---. "Madness, Distress and Postmodernity: Putting the Record Straight." *Disability/Postmodernity: Embodying Disability Theory*. Ed. Mairian Corker and Tom Shakespeare. London: Continuum, 2002. 143-58.

Cartwright, Samuel. "Report on the Diseases and Physical Peculiarities of the Negro Race." Part 1. *New Orleans Medical and Surgical Journal* 8 (1851): 692-713.

Campbell, Bebe Moore. *72 Hour Hold*. New York: Alfred A. Knopf, 2005.

Canning, Christopher. "Psychiatric Survivor Testimonials and Embodiment: Emotional Challenges to Medical Knowledge." *Radical Psychology* 5 (Winter 2006): 37 pars. 10 Jan. 2008 <http://www.radpsynet.org/journal/vol5/Canning.html>.

Davis, Lennard J. Introduction. *The Disability Studies Reader*. 2nd ed. Ed. Lennard J. Davis. New York: Routledge, 2006. xv-xviii.

Donaldson, Elizabeth J. "The Corpus of the Madwoman: Toward a Feminist Disability Studies Theory of Embodiment and Mental Illness." *NWSA* 14.3 (2002): 99-119.

Felman, Shoshana. "Women and Madness: The Critical Phallacy." *Feminisms: An Anthology of Literary Theory and Criticism*. Ed. Robyn R. Warhol and Diane Price Herndl. New Brunswick, NJ: Rutgers UP, 1997. 7-20.

Fox, Margalit. "Bebe Moore Campbell, Novelist of Black Lives, Dies at 56." *The New York Times* 28 November 2006. 15 pars. 15 March 2008 <http://www.nytimes.com/2006/11/28/books/28campbell.html?_r=1&oref=slogin>.

Gilman, Sander L. *Difference and Pathology: Stereotypes of Sexuality, Race, and Madness*. Ithaca: Cornell UP, 1985.

Ingram, Richard. "Reports from the Psych Wars." *Unfitting Stories: Narrative Approaches to Disease, Disability, and Trauma*. Ed. Valerie Raoul, et al. Waterloo, ON: Wilfred Laurier UP, 2007. 237-45.

Jackson, Vanessa. "In Our Own Voice: African-American Stories of
    Oppression, Survival and Recovery in Mental Health Systems." Online
    manuscript. 15 Jan. 2008 <http://dsmc.info/pdf/voices.pdf>.

Marks, Deborah. "Healing the Split between Psyche and Social: Constructions
    and Experiences of Disability." *Disability Studies Quarterly* 22.3 (2002):
    46-52.

Mitchell, David T. and Sharon L. Snyder. "Introduction: Disability Studies and
    the Double Bind of Representation." *The Body and Physical Difference:
    Discourses of Disability*. Ed. David T. Mitchell and Sharon L. Snyder.
    Ann Arbor: U of Michigan P, 1997. 1-34.

---. *Narrative Prosthesis: Disability and the Dependencies of Discourse*. Ann
    Arbor: U of Michigan P, 2000.

Mollow, Anna. "'When *Black* Women Start Going on Prozac': Race, Gender,
    and Mental Illness in Meri Nana-Ama Danquah's *Willow Weep for Me*."
    MELUS 31.3 (2006): 67-99.

Nicki, Andrea. "The Abused Mind: Feminist Theory, Psychiatric Disability, and
    Trauma." *Hypatia* 16.4 (Fall 2001): 80-104.

Patterson, Orlando. *Slavery and Social Death: A Comparative Study*.
    Cambridge: Harvard UP, 1982.

Prendergast, Catherine. "On the Rhetorics of Mental Disability." *Embodied
    Rhetorics: Disability in Language and Culture*. Ed. James C. Wilson and
    Cynthia Lewiecki-Wilson. Carbondale, IL: Southern Illinois UP, 2001.
    45-60.

Rosen, George. *Madness in Society: Chapters in the Historical Sociology of
    Mental Illness*. Chicago: U of Chicago P, 1968.

Cassandra Jackson

Visualizing Slavery: Photography and the Disabled Subject in the Art of Carrie Mae Weems

In 1863 the photography firm of McPherson & Oliver of Baton Rouge produced at least two photographs of a man called Gordon.[1] In both photos, Gordon sits with his bare back facing the camera; clusters of dense ropelike scars extend across his back. At the time, the subject's nudity alone would have made the photographs remarkable, but the dreadful mutilation at the center of these images is what claims the viewer's attention. One of the photographs was later published as a carte de visite by McAllister Brothers of Philadelphia and titled "The Scourged Back" (Fig. 3.1.). This photograph is believed to have been widely circulated in the nineteenth century and was reproduced at least one other time in the United States and again in England.[2] It also appeared as part of a triptych of engravings in *Harper's Weekly* that same year and in an English broadside published the following year.[3] While the life of the other untitled photograph is not as well known, the various versions of the image, with different versos, suggest that it too was reproduced and circulated[4] (Fig. 3.2.). In the late twentieth and early twenty-first centuries, both images have appeared in countless forms of media including historical documentaries, internet websites, textbooks, and even a CD cover, making these photographs perhaps the most widely viewed and circulated images of a slave.

Numerous contemporary African American artists, including Michael Harris, Robert Pruitt, and Hank Willis Thomas, reflect on and incorporate these images into their work. In this essay, I want to discuss how Carrie Mae Weems encounters the untitled photograph in her art. Weems integrates the photograph into a print, *Black and Tanned* (1995) (Fig. 3.3.). Her use of this photograph leads viewers towards conceptual engagement with slavery and its contemporary implications. Her works function, to use Brian Massumi's term, as a "a shock to thought," or rather what Jill Bennett calls "a jolt that does not so much reveal truth as thrust us involuntarily into a mode of critical inquiry" (11). Thus, her work does not attempt to reveal slavery's truth in as much as it propels viewers towards critical explorations of the legacies of slavery.

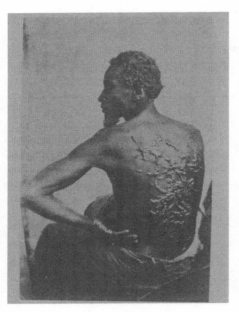 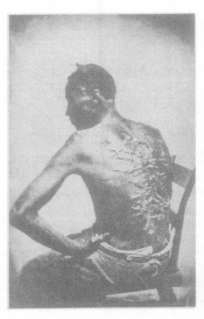

Fig. 3.1. *The Scourged Back*, photograph of Gordon, an escaped slave (1863). Prints and Photographs Division, Schomburg Center for Research in Black Culture, The New York Public Library, Astor, Lenox, and Tilden Foundations. Used by permission.

Fig. 3.2. "Overseer Artayou Carrier whipped me. I was two months in bed sore from the whipping. My master come after I was whipped; he discharged the overseer. The very words of poor Peter, taken as he sat for his picture. Baton Rouge, Louisiana, 04/02/1863." The National Archives at College Park. Used by permission.

Through the appropriation of this photograph, the artist encounters two central problems of putting the disabled body on display: "Disability" as Lennard Davis argues "is a specular moment," and thus the visual experience of encountering the disabled body enacts, "the power of the gaze to control, limit, and patrol the disabled person" (12). At the same time the viewing of disability is always narrative, or as Davis puts it: "A person became deaf, became blind, was born blind, became quadriplegic" (3). Therefore, disability is often reduced to a "chronotype, a time-sequenced narrative," which is itself a means of controlling the meaning of disability (ibid.). Indeed, as Davis contends, "by narrativizing an impairment, one tends to sentimentalize it and link it to the bourgeois sensibility of individualism and the drama of an individual story" (ibid.).

Fig. 3.3. Carrie Mae Weems, *Black and Tanned your Whipped Wind of Change Howled Low Blowing Itself-Ha –Smack Into the Middle of Ellington's Orchestra Billie Heard it too & Cried Strange Fruit Tears* (1995) from the series *From Here I Saw What Happened and I Cried, 1995*. Courtesy of the artist and the Jack Shainman Gallery.

In the case of the black wounded body, these issues of the power of the gaze and the reductiveness of narrative are magnified. Because the black body is never individual, but instead is always the representative of the collective other, the image of the disabled black body extends beyond the singular to become emblematic. What is being monitored and storied is not a single body, but a collective body. Thus, the meaning of disability in this case is indelibly entangled in the meaning of blackness, both its ideological meaning and the ways in which it manifest materially as a violated body. The narrative of what happened is reduced to: He is a slave; slaves are beaten; beatings equal slavery. The story then not only compresses the individual into a chronological narrative explanation, but it compresses the history of slavery into a single defining narrative. Indeed, this view is what explains the photographic reproduction of the image. The photograph functions to sum up the meaning of slavery, and thus blackness.

To address this issue, Weems confronts the problems of the photographic medium itself, and more precisely its tendency to exploit the disabled black subject. Weems's manipulation of the photograph attempts to expose and address the problems of putting the wounded body of the slave on display by shifting our attention from the body as a discrete object, to the body and the photograph itself as sites of complex ideological struggle. As Davis points out, "the body generally [...] has been conceptualized as a simple object when it is in fact a complex focus for competing power structures" (11). Similarly, photography has often been viewed as transparent truth, rather than a sophisticated mode of representation. By exposing the socio-historical forces that shape the photograph itself, Weems shifts the viewers' attention from the disabled body to the larger trajectories of competing power structures that shape the image.

Weems way of resisting the problems of the medium is through the interjection of the figure of trauma into her work. *Black and Tanned* collapses time frames, rejecting chronological histories for a palimpsest mode of expression that recalls both the idea of traumatic memory as well as that of testimony. As it collapses the distant past, the not so distant past, and the present, it evokes the primary mechanism of trauma, its invasive recurring memories that know no distinctions of time. The evocation of traumatic memory invests Weems's art with multitemporal modes of representation, and thus calls critical attention to linear narratives, or rather the limits of historiography. Summoning the effect of trauma then becomes a means to disavow the photograph's depiction of the wounded black body as a static, explicable, historical object that encapsulates slavery and blackness. *Black and Tanned* acknowledges the way in which the trauma of slavery remains outside of the domain of linear narratives, while nonetheless theorizing visual testimonies that bear witness to the collective trauma of slavery.

Abolitionism and the Disabled Black Subject

As she encounters the photograph, Weems confronts its exploitive implications. Shaped by a repressive nineteenth-century ideological terrain, the original photograph equates blackness with wounded, viewable, legible bodies. Indeed, as it exposes the scars that even the subject cannot see, the photograph offers the observer the power to view and interpret the body. This emphasis on the body demonstrates how the "mute testimony" of the photograph also overrides the testimony of the slave, making the slave's voice superfluous, unnecessary. The photograph privileges what Hortense Spillers calls, the "hieroglyphics of the flesh," and thus the body, the master's writing on the body, countermands the voice of the slave, while also creating an elision between the viewer and the master (67).

This relationship is ultimately exacerbated by the eroticism of the photograph. Such nudity at a time when photographic subjects were shrouded in layers of clothing and props is fraught with prurient voyeurism. Indeed, that the viewer can see his back, which even the subject cannot see, speaks to these voyeuristic impulses. In addition, the composition of the image, the graceful angles and turns of the body, encourages a sensual experience for the viewer. The three-dimensionality of the scars promotes an almost tactile experience. Moreover, the overall outline of the image, created by the outer points of the body, the sharply angled elbow, the supple slope of the right shoulder, encourage the viewer's eye to roam about the body, tracing its outline, while the sumptuous opening between the arm and the torso, encourage the eye to enter the bodies voids. This eroticism recalls the legacy of slavery: the multifaceted ways in which commodified bodies are by virtue of this commodification overembodied. Thus, the photograph also maps a disturbing parallelism between slavery and photography, in that in both the black body functions as a commodity to be endlessly bought and sold. The appropriative impulses of photography have been explored extensively, but this photograph in particular makes plain the short distance between the auction block and the posing stand, the slave collar and the positioning neck clamp.

The photograph of the disabled black subject would have also had disturbing narrative implications for nineteenth-century viewers. For them, this specular experience of the wounded black male body would have also been associated with popular narratives of black disability that had become a familiar part of antislavery literature and imagery. Indeed, when the 1863 photograph emerged, the figure of the wounded black male slave was well known among American audiences. Its most famous portrayal was the biggest selling novel of the nineteenth century, Harriet Beecher Stowe's *Uncle Tom's Cabin* (1851). Because the book was translated widely into engravings, stage dramas, dolls, art, and other mediums, even the illiterate would have been familiar with Stowe's tale of the faithful, childlike slave whose noble body was beaten to death.

According to Marianne Noble, such accounts of torture and mutilation participated in "sentimental wounding" or the effort to provoke "a bodily experience of anguish caused by identification with another's pain" (295). Such representations aimed to spark an intuitive understanding of the importance of the abolitionist cause and move the audience to participate in antislavery activism. The narrative that produced this effect of identification and transference was a narrative of disability, in which the slave is mutilated. Thus, this notion of "sentimental wounding" operated on the premise that viewing the disabled body would spark an empathic experience, and thus transfer that body's pain to the audience. In other words, viewing disability would cause the audience to feel their own bodily vulnerability. As Davis points out, "the disabled body is always the reminder of the whole body about to come apart at the seams" (132). Thus "sentimental wounding," functioned as a way of narrativizing the disabled body, and ultimately controlling its meaning. In the antislavery context black disability was intended to spark feelings of bodily vulnerability in a white able-bodied audience, and at the same time the narrative offered that audience the opportunity to intervene in disability through activism.

The1863 photograph visualizes this process of sentimental wounding, offering up the exposed and wounded slave body not only to shock viewers, but to provoke identification with the subject's pain. Like the literary sentimental narratives that Noble refers to, the photograph encouraged viewers to appropriate that pain by viscerally translating it from a visual experience to a bodily one, all to induce support for the anti-slavery cause. The 1863 photograph would have been part of a prepackaged cultural narrative of disability in which the wounded black body functions as a means through which an able-bodied white audience could vicariously experience the bodily pain of the mutilated slave, while also being empowered to ameliorate that pain via activism.

The imagery of the wounded slave was part of a series of conventions with pre-established meanings. The narrative of wounding allows for control over the subject, or rather the meaning of the disability through narrative. As Jane Tompkins, Karen Sanchez-Eppler, and others have argued, sentimental narratives operate through stereotypes, figures that can signify meaning in a condensed form. Such stereotypes center on the readability of bodies: "the self is externally displayed, and the body provides a reliable sign of who one is" (Sanchez-Eppler 36). Sentiment then makes bodies legible, knowable, sufficient sources of knowledge. Thus, for the nineteenth-century audience, the body of the wounded slave would have been a knowable, readable object made legible in the context of the culture of sentiment.

"Sentimental wounding" encourages what Bertolt Brecht terms "crude empathy," a sentiment produced by the assimilation of another's experiences as one's own (Bennett 10). By inviting the viewer to share the subject's pain and suggesting that the body might be a conduit to establish connectivity between the viewer and the subject, the 1863 photograph encounters the dangers of the empathic impulse, at once appropriative and disaffecting. Oddly, while it invites the viewer to share in experiencing the body of the subject, it also reinscribes otherness by demanding the exploitation of the black disabled body. Abolitionist sentiment here relies on the mutilated body. As Saadiya Hartman points out, "The slave was considered a subject only in so far as he was criminalized, wounded body or mortified flesh" (94). Thus, black subjectivity depends on the brutalized body.

Confronting Photography
By adopting the 1863 photograph, Weems confronts these issues of appropriation and exploitation. Yet, she initiates this encounter by also appropriating the photograph and the torn body of the slave. Cast in red tone, *Black and Tanned* repeats the original untitled image of the slave facing left with his back turned to the camera. But Weems's large chromogenic color print of the image also offers striking contrasts to the tiny original carte de visite. The print is cast in red and includes dark shadows that fall on the body. While the viewer can still see the figure of the man's body and make out the scar tissue, the red and black cast blurs the details of the body. The face, for example, is darkened so much that its edges are as black as a silhouette cutout. The image is also framed and surrounded by a circular black mat. Finally the lower half of the image is covered in text, which is sandblasted onto the glass enclosure. It reads,

BLACK AND TANNED / YOUR WHIPPED WIND / OF CHANGE HOWLED LOW / BLOWING ITSELF-HA-SMACK INTO THE MIDDLE OF ELLINGTON'S ORCHESTRA / BILLIE HEARD IT TOO & / CRIED STRANGE FRUIT TEARS

Black and Tanned exposes the ubiquitous role of photography in the creation of cultural memory and the demarcation of the black subject through formal techniques that make visible the photographic process. The mat with its circular opening calls our attention to the camera lens, placing the viewer behind the camera. Speaking of this effect, Weems points out that she "wanted to have that sense of looking through the photographic lens [because] when we're looking at the images we are looking at the ways in which Anglo-America, white America, saw itself in relationship to the black subject" (Museum of Modern Art). Thus, Weems not only evokes the presence of the camera, but by placing the viewer in the place of the photographer she calls critical attention to the ways in which the camera was implicated in the dehumanization of black people. Interestingly, the place of the photographer, the viewer, and that of the abuser are all one in the same, an elision that compounds the tension between past and present, while also clarifying the way in which the photograph extends beyond such boundaries. Though Weems started her career as a documentary photographer, she soon became concerned with the power implications of the genre, especially its tendency to afford viewers a sense of mastery over subjects, including disempowered black subjects (Collins, *The Art of History* 30). Weems's continued interest in and contention with documentary photography is evident in her work. As Thomas Piché has pointed out, "she plays with the idea of documentary photography, subverting, even while appropriating, the authority of the genre" (10). Cherise Smith adds that Weems's use of historical documentary photography in her work serves to reclaim "the dignity and pride that whites attempted to wrest – through stereotyping and mistreatment – from individuals of African descent" (119).

Weems's 1995 exhibit *From Here I Saw What Happened and I Cried,* the larger exhibit in which *Black and Tanned* was included, demonstrates this way in which she grapples not only with documentary photography, but with portraiture, anthropological photography, indeed, with photography itself as an expressive and sometimes oppressive medium. The exhibit was commissioned as a response to the J. Paul Getty Museum's exhibit "Hidden Witness: African Americans in Early Photography," an exhibition of rare photographs of African-Americans taken between the 1840s and the 1860's. Upon an invitation to explore the Getty Museum's photography collection, Weems selected photographs of black men and women from the collection as well as others, re-photographed them, toned the prints in red, matted and framed them. The overall exhibit as Thelma Golden has argued, "created an alternative history that simultaneously embraced and rejected what the museum's photographs represented. Instead of simply exhibiting one of her own previous pieces, she […] critically read the museum's show through her own new series of works" (29-30).

From Here I Saw What Happened and I Cried (1995) operates as a critical intervention into the history of photography, exploring the relationship between photography and black subjectivity. Beginning with what could be read as an anthropological photograph of a West African woman cast in blue tone, followed by the infamous typological Agassiz daguerreotypes of nude South Carolina slaves cast in red tone, the series implicates photography in the pseudoscience of racial classification. Lest her viewers miss this point, the text on the glass enclosures of the four Agassiz daguerreotypes reads successively "YOU BECAME A SCIENTIFIC PROFILE / A NEGROID TYPE / AN ANTHROPOLOGICAL DEBATE / & A PHOTOGRAPHIC SUBJECT." Thus, by clarifying this equation between the black subject and the racial type, the text announces the way in which photography itself is not only inextricable from, but was also actively engaged in, establishing and maintaining a racialized sociopolitical landscape. The images also articulate the initiation of a critical exploration of photography's capacity to shape and diminish black subjectivity. Significantly, this exploration includes photographs dating beyond the time frame of the "Hidden Witness" exhibit, and extending through the nineteenth and twentieth centuries. Thus, the series bridges time periods shifting away from a sense of chronology to invest in a more multisynchronous form of expression. This treatment of time not only resists the view of the photograph as an unmediated purveyor of historical knowledge, it also envelops it in a kind of temporal cloudiness that speaks to its place as part of the larger cultural memory. Extending beyond fixed periods of time, the series suggest the ways in which the photographs themselves cannot be contained by temporal boundaries.

Black and Tanned also intervenes in this process through its treatment of the body. More specifically, Weems's work experiments with ways of taking the body back from the exploitative mechanisms of photography. The mats then serve a dual function. At the same time that they call our attention to the camera the mats control and limit the gaze, concealing parts of the head, lower back, and legs. Weems's print controls the eye of the viewer, limiting the gaze by presenting and yet withholding the subject's body at once to challenge the power implications of the original photograph. Imparting both somberness and dignity, the mat quietly and protectively encloses the image, withdrawing it from the viewer. In addition, the darkening of the face insists on the collective significance of the image. While the print is treated with the intimacy of a family photograph, embracing the subject in the circle, it also presents the subject as broadly symbolic of African-American experiences. Indeed, if, as Smith has argued, the red tone suggests blood, then Weems's choice to cast the prints in the series in red creates a symbolic bodily connection between them (Smith 119).

Trauma and Testimony as Intervention

As she confronts the oppressive implications of photography through the very same medium, Weems risks reinscribing those implications. In this way, she encounters a problem similar to that encountered by authors of neo-slave narratives who work within the context of a medium that has been implicated in the formation of racial hierarchy. These writers contend with the ways in which literacy itself "was so thoroughly implicated in the definitions of humanity, reason, and culture that bolstered the institution of slavery" (Dubey 195). In the preface to her novel *Dessa Rose* (1986), Sherley Anne Williams declares that black people have been "betrayed" by literature and writing (5). Thus, she and other writers employ strategies that, as Madhu Dubey points out, attempt to "disavow the literate and literary mode that forms each author's chosen medium of expression" (187). For Toni Morrison this has meant that her writing endeavors to be "not [...] merely literary" but instead, contain an ability to speak to "an illiterate or preliterate reader" ("Memory" 387). According to Dubey, Morrison's fiction attempts to be an "anti-literature" that draws not so much on the formal conventions of the novel, as on the vernacular traditions of African-American culture (188). Indeed, Morrison has maintained that her writing aims "to be like something that has probably only been fully expressed perhaps in music" (McKay 426). The incorporation of the vernacular serves to both disavow the literary and to facilitate multitemporal spaces that can more fully express the experiences of slavery. Dubey asserts, "The overlapping dimensions of the oral thus achieve a perfect identification between the generations, obliterating the breaks and discontinuities entailed by the history of slavery and restoring an immediate full presence" (193).

Like these writers of the neoslave narrative, Weems engages in critical practices that acknowledge the problems of the medium while also trying to make meaning through that medium. The similarities between the problems of representation that these literary and visual artists encounter is evidenced in the fact that members of both groups use strategies that privilege the vernacular to reject linear histories in favor of these "overlapping dimensions." Thomas Piché has described Weems's incorporation of texts into her work as a "visual analog" to the speakerly text – a written text that privileges the oral. "In effect" he writes, "Weems's photographs are double voiced, standing as visual images with multivalent meaning but functioning as well as semantic entities that give visual form to the rhetorical strategies found in the text" (15-16).

The visual strategies of Weems's work are closely aligned with these rhetorical strategies. Just as the authors access the preliterate as a rejection of the literary, the artist explores traumatic memory – a non-artistic experience of the visual – as a critique of photography, this supposed medium of objective truth. *Black and Tanned* conveys trauma by registering the effect of the flashback. The strange clarity and yet graininess of the photograph, unlike the tactile effect of the original photograph, serves to distance the image, situating it in the past, while the clarity of the image as it emerges from the red tone establishes its presence. Piché notes that: "[Weems] likes a rolliflex lens because it gives clarity to the photographic subject but yields a slightly soft focus that implies a sense of past time – something a little old, but still contemporary" (10). This effect maintains a constant tension between past and present, while it also registers the effect of the flashback because at its center is this visual echo, surfacing in clarity and withdrawing into the graininess. This effect initiates and enunciates the encounter with the traumatic event referenced by the original photograph. And yet the elusiveness of the photograph familiar, yet fading, clear, yet veiled, like a memory suggests its unreliability as a record of the event. Thus, the image validates the visual experience of traumatic memory, while also challenging any notion of unmediated historicity. Trauma in this instance then is not about the individual subjective experience but a site of critical encounter that theorizes the visuality of cultural memory.

Weems's representation of the visuality of traumatic experience reveals both the inadequacy of the nineteenth-century photograph's display of the wounded body in conveying the experiences of slavery and blackness, as well as the way in which our understanding of slavery and black subjectivity is shaped by the photograph. Lisa Saltzman and Eric Rosenberg state the relationship between trauma and the visual thus:

The formulation of trauma as discourse is predicated upon metaphors of visuality and image as unavoidable carrier of the unrepresentable. From primal scene to flashback to screen memory to the dream, much of the language deployed to speak trauma's character is emphatically if not exclusively, visual. It may even be argued that the very form taken by trauma as a phenomenon is only, however, asymptotically or not, understood as or when pictured. (xi-xii)

Weems's work taps into this idea of the visuality of trauma, and by doing so her art challenges the idea of the photograph itself as readable historical object. That is, her work acknowledges the photograph as having been integrated into the psychovisual, as itself a construction shaped by and shaping cultural memory.

Morrison's *Beloved* (1987) illuminates the ways in which the representation of the visual nature of traumatic experience operates as a strategy that disempowers linear histories. Indeed, the novel signals a connection between the visual and the oral as strategies that resist official histories when Sethe narrates for Denver the concept of "rememory":

What I remember is a picture floating around out there outside my head. I mean, even if I don't think it, even if I die, the picture of what I did, or knew, or saw is still out there. Right in the place where it happened. [...] Someday you be walking down the road and you hear something or see something going on. So clear. And you think it's you thinking it up. A thought picture. But no. It's when you bump into a rememory that belongs to somebody else. (43)

Sethe describes the experience of "rememory," as an intense encounter with living pictures that float independent of their owners, irrespective of the passing of time. In this way, Morrison captures not only the visuality of memory, but the very nature of trauma for as Bruce Simon explains, "Trauma is about the literal return [...] of a painful or catastrophic event" (104). This concept of "rememory," also demonstrates the distance between experience and history, or rather the failure of history to elucidate the experience of slavery. Thus, the vernacular and the psycho-visual in the novel function as ways of resisting the authority of sanctioned histories by expressing these overlapping time frames and floating pictures that capture the thorny workings of memory.

The representation of traumatic memory in Weems's art also uses the psycho-visual as a strategy that resists the linear narration of the disabled body. More specifically, by evoking the 1863 photograph that seems at once present and distant, *Black and Tanned* privileges this visual experience of memory over the photograph as historical object. This effect functions in multiple and sometimes competing ways. By rejecting the photograph as historical artifact, the piece calls attention to the problems of the photographic practice, the ways in which photography has been used to craft blackness, to delimit slavery, and shape black subjectivity. In addition, it acknowledges the inescapable power of photography, its ability to construct and shape collective memory, for as Marianne Hirsch points out, memory is made up of representation (8). Furthermore, by centering on the photographed body, it recognizes the centrality of the body in this construction of memory, while also challenging the notion of the body as a sufficient source of knowledge. By calling attention to photographic practice this effect reminds us that the photographed body is constructed through visual means. Thus, while her art interrogates the medium, it also acknowledges it as a ubiquitous force that gives shape and form to slavery, blackness, and memory – a force that even her own work cannot escape.

The text imposed on the glass enclosure also dramatically reconfigures the original image, transforming trauma into a testimonial act. By placing the manipulated 1863 photograph in the context of African-American artistic production, more specifically the music of Duke Ellington and Billie Holiday, Weems integrates the body of the subject into a narrative of collective African-American transformation that testifies to the translation of such horrors, such trauma, into the birth of jazz. That the text reads "your whipped wind of change" rather than your whipped back places emphasis on transformation, rather than on the moment of violence, and thus prevents the reenactment of the violation by insisting on projecting the image into a future engendered by the experiences that the image represents. This effect is compounded by ways in which the text uses orality to signal the testimonial mode. More specifically, the text privileges orality and the vernacular by focusing on auditory experiences. The words "WHIPPED WIND," "HOWLED LOW," "HA-SMACK," and "BILLIE HEARD IT TOO," all center on auditory experience, whether through alliteration, onomatopoeia, or the narration of something heard. Furthermore, this emphasis on the testimonial is amplified by the way in which the words function as part of the visual experience, preventing the tendency to read the body. Instead, the eyes must pass over the image, reading the words from left to right, privileging the act of testimony over the interpretation of the body. Significantly, the text is sandblasted into the glass enclosure, a process that suggests force and yet is based on a natural process of erosion. It is as if the violence referenced by the image, the violent act of writing on the body, can only be interrupted by a violent act of revision. In this way the sandblasted texts enunciates her intervention, while the practice of sandblasting itself echoes the words "whipped wind of change."

Weems's translation of the disfigured form of the subject into a collective source of inspiration and invention operates as an act of testimony. The testimonial mode is particularly apt here because as Anne Cubilié and Carl Good point out, testimony is not a fixed or formulaic process, but instead allows for multidimensional, multigenerational modes of representation. Mapping cartographies of experience, across time and space, *Black and Tanned* bears witness to the past and its effects that reverberate well into the twentieth century. If as trauma studies suggest "trauma signals a breakdown in the historical conditions through which subjects know and narrate their experience," requiring "a more figurative testimonial agency to world it back into existence," one might think of *Black and Tanned* as filling the gaps between history and experience, chronology and consciousness (Harkins 139). Weems's art demonstrates how the testimonial mode offers ways of "bearing witness to the unrepresentable" (Cubilié and Good 5).

Weems's treatment of trauma demonstrates how the representation of trauma is not about equating black subjectivity with black victimization. Instead, *Black and Tanned* demonstrates how the idea of traumatic memory affords ways of challenging such ideologies, while also acknowledging the presence of the past. As Bruce Simon notes, part of the usefulness of theorizing slavery as a trauma is that the very notion of trauma allows for ways of figuring the sufferer as a survivor of trauma. *Black and Tanned* maps broad notions of survival, not merely that of the individual, but cultural, collective, artistic, and testimonial survivals. By evoking the idea of traumatic memory, the artist demonstrates that slavery or the trauma of slavery cannot be represented by a single disfigured body, but instead "is about […] the recurrence and the survival of a painful catastrophic event or experience" (Simon 104). At the same time, the notion of traumatic memory affords ways of challenging a political landscape that dismisses the impact of slavery on the now because trauma poses serious challenges to those who want to dismiss slavery's impact on the present (ibid.). Indeed the very notion of traumatic memory demonstrates how the past remains in tension with the present (Bennett 11).

[1] An article entitled "A Typical Negro" published in *Harper's Weekly* refers to the man pictured as Gordon. See Anon. On the verso of another carte that pictures the same man, he is called Peter. This carte is held by the U.S. National Archives and includes a short narrative of the events surrounding the beating that supposedly resulted in the scars pictured. The narrative concludes with the line, "The very words of poor Peter, taken as he sat for his picture." See Fig. 3.2.

[2] According Kathleen Collins the image was reproduced by C. Seaver of Boston, Massachusetts. She notes that a British copy of the image published by Fred Jones Photo of 146 Oxford St. was found among the papers of Henry Ward Beecher. For more information see Collins, "The Scourged Black."

[3] For a discussion of these print media reproductions of this image, see Wood 266-71.

[4] This untitled carte is sometimes mislabeled as "The Scourged Back," though the carte itself does not bear that title.

Works Cited

Anon. "A Typical Negro." *Harper's Weekly* 4 July 1863. 429-30.

Bennett, Jill. *Empathic Vision: Affect, Trauma, and Contemporary Art*. Stanford: Stanford UP, 2005.

Collins, Kathleen. "The Scourged Back." *History of Photography* 9.1 (1985): 43-45.

Collins, Lisa Gail. *The Art of History: African American Women Artists Engage the Past*. New Brunswick, NJ: Rutgers UP, 2002.

Cubilié, Anne, and Carl Good. "Introduction: The Future of Testimony." *Discourse* 25.1 (2001): 4-18.

Davis, Lennard J. *Enforcing Normalcy: Disability, Deafness, and the Body*. New York: Verso, 1995.

Dubey, Madhu. "The Politics of Genre in *Beloved*." *Novel* 32.2 (1999): 187-206.

Golden, Thelma. "Some Thoughts on Carrie Mae Weems." *Carrie Mae Weems: Recent Work, 1992-1998*. Ed. Thomas Piché Jr. and Thelma Golden. New York: George Braziller, 1998. 29-34.

Harkins, Gillian. "Seduction by Law: Sexual Property and Testimonial Possession in *Thereafter Johnnie*." *Discourse* 25.1 (2003): 138-65.

Hartman, Saidiya V. *Scenes of Subjection: Terror, Slavery, and Self-Making in Nineteenth-Century America*. New York: Oxford UP, 1997.

Hirsch, Marianne. "Surviving Images: Holocaust Photographs and the Work of
    Postmemory." *The Yale Journal of Criticism* 14.1 (2001): 5-37.

Massumi, Brian. *A Shock to Thought: Expressions after Deleuze and Guattari.*
    New York: Routledge, 2002.

Morrison, Toni. *Beloved.* New York: Vintage, 1987.

---. Interview with Nellie McKay. *Contemporary Literature* 24.4 (1983): 413-
    29.

---. "Memory, Creation, and Writing." *Thought* 59 (Dec. 1984): 385-90.

Museum of Modern Art. Interview with Carrie Mae Weems. *MOMA: The
    Collection.* Audio Program Excerpt from the Exhibition "Out of Time: A
    Contemporary View, 30 Aug. 2006 – 9 Apr. 2007." 14 Feb. 2007 <http://
    www.moma.org/collection/browse_results.php?criteria=O%3AAD%3AE
    %3A7177&page_number=1&template_id=1&sort_order=1>.

Noble, Marianne. "The Ecstasies of Sentimental Wounding in *Uncle Tom's
    Cabin.*" *The Yale Journal of Criticism* 10.2 (1997): 295-320.

Piché, Thomas. "Reading Carrie Mae Weems." *Carrie Mae Weems: Recent
    Work, 1992-1998.* Ed. Thomas Piché Jr. and Thelma Golden. New York:
    George Braziller, 1998. 9-27.

Saltzman, Lisa, and Eric M. Rosenberg. Introduction. *Trauma and Visuality in
    Modernity.* Ed. Lisa Saltzman and Eric M. Rosenberg. Hanover, NH:
    Dartmouth College P, 2006. ix-xix.

Sanchez-Eppler, Karen. "Bodily Bonds: The Intersecting Rhetorics of Feminism
    and Abolition." *Representations* 24 (Fall 1988): 28-59.

Simon, Bruce. "Traumatic Repetition in Gayl Jones's *Corregidora.*" *Race
    Consciousness: African-American Studies for the New Century.* Ed. Judith
    Jackson Fossett and Jeffrey A. Tucker. New York: New York UP, 1997.
    93-112.

Smith, Cherise. "Fragmented Documents: Works by Lorna Simpson, Carrie Mae
    Weems and Willie Robert Middlebrook at the Art Institute of Chicago."
    African Americans in Art: Selections from the Art Institute of Chicago.
    Ed. Susan F. N. L. Rosen. Seattle: The U of Washington P, 1999. 245-59.

Spillers, Hortense. "Mama's Baby, Papa's Maybe: An American Grammar
    Book." *Diacritics* 17.2 (1987): 65-81.

Williams, Sherley Anne. *Dessa Rose.* New York: William Morrow, 1986.

Wood, Marcus. *Blind Memory: Visual Representations of Slavery in England
    and America.* New York: Routledge, 2000.

Stella Bolaki

Challenging Invisibility, Making Connections: Illness, Survival, and Black Struggles in Audre Lorde's Work

> Wherever the bird with no feet flew she found trees with no limbs.
>
> (*Zami* 31)

In her essay "Integrating Disability, Transforming Feminist Theory," Rosemarie Garland-Thomson argues that "integrating disability does not obscure our critical focus on the registers of race, sexuality, ethnicity, or gender, nor is it additive." Rather, "considering disability shifts the conceptual framework to strengthen our understanding of how these multiple systems intertwine, redefine, and mutually constitute one another." As she explains further, "Integrating disability clarifies how this aggregate of systems operates together, yet distinctly, to support an imaginary norm and structure the relations that grant power, privilege, and status to that norm" (4). Garland-Thomson specifically addresses, here, the need to start using disability as a category of analysis in feminist studies, but her statement serves at the same time to point out the benefits that arise from a consideration of the interrelationships between disability and race, ethnicity, or sexuality in literary and cultural studies. While in the last decade, disability studies theories and methodologies have become popular in the humanities, starting to inform feminist, but also, more recently, queer theory (see 2002 *GLQ* special issue), there is little work that considers intersections between disability and race. An exception is the 2006 Pre-Conference on Race, Ethnicity, and Disability coordinated by the Society for Disability Studies, which convened in Bethesda, Maryland, and the *MELUS* special issue "Race, Ethnicity, Disability, and Literature: Intersections and Interventions" which appeared in 2006. Without other sustained efforts to investigate similar encounters, it is hard not to agree with Chris Bell that "we are still positioned in the realm of 'White Disability Studies'" (281).

Audre Lorde's work has been a starting point for me, as it has been for others, when it comes to thinking about and addressing the ways in which the categories of race, sexuality, and disability/illness constitute one another. In her work, Lorde grounds any examination of the relationship of the self to the world in "the geography closest in, the body" (Rich 212) and encourages us to think about how certain practices of discrimination have kept seemingly different people in similar marginalized positions. Throughout her life, Lorde used different aspects of her identity (female, black, lesbian, poet, mother, cancer survivor, to mention just a few) as passports to enter several sisterhoods and communities both inside and outside the boundaries of America.

This essay examines her work within a disability studies framework, focusing on *Zami: A New Spelling of My Name* (1982), *The Cancer Journals* (1980), and "A Burst of Light: Living with Cancer" (1988). There is so much narrative overspill between these texts that I am tempted to describe Lorde's life narrative in linear terms, as involving the following stages: learning how to survive while growing up black and lesbian in America, using these lessons of survival in order to approach and make sense of her subsequent experience with cancer, and proceeding to teach other people how to break the silence and turn personal struggles into politically useful ones. Though Lorde uses the past to understand the present in the case of dealing with breast and liver cancer, this process is not one-way. Illness considerably changes her writing and activism, becoming, in Arthur Frank's phrase, an occasion for "the renewal of generosity" (1) in that it forces her to stretch further and to reflect on her responsibilities towards black diasporic women all over the world (specifically in "Burst of Light"). Just as in her cancer journals illness and race constitute one another, *Zami* documents mutual processes by revealing how disability has always been racialised and how race has been conceived as disability. In the sections that follow, I trace such convergences between race and disability, or illness, race, lesbian sexuality, and class, as well as connections between illness and struggles in a more transnational context. There are, of course, certain moments, as I suggest, when race seems to elide a focus on illness or disability, but Lorde never seems to succumb to crude simplifications that conflate disability with race and vice versa. In most cases, oppositional subjectivity emerges from the encounter of disability with race and queerness as in the memorable figure of the Dahomean single-breasted amazons, which embody a kind of triple consciousness for Lorde (black, lesbian, and disabled).

To be sure, Lorde's *Cancer Journals* has been a constant reference point in studies on illness narratives that take either a narratological or cultural studies perspective (such as Frank's *Wounded Storyteller*, and David B. Morris's *Illness and Culture in the Postmodern Age*), as well as in studies on breast cancer and what Jeanne Perreault has called "feminist autography." Such studies, though they recognize the difference of Lorde's narrative from white, heterosexual, middle-class experiences of illness, ultimately use her story of resistance (in particular her powerful attack against prosthesis) to trace an important moment when patients refuse to surrender to medical authority and reclaim the capacity to tell their own stories. While this is part of what Lorde does, she also seeks, as she writes in *The Cancer Journals*, to explore how her "experiences with cancer fit into the larger tapestry of my work as a Black woman" (10). A critic who has explored Lorde's work through an approach that is sensitive to both race and disability is Garland-Thomson in her study *Extraordinary Bodies*. More specifically, she historicizes *Zami* (together with novels by Toni Morrison and Ann Petry) suggesting that their anti-assimilationist gesture and celebration of difference stem from a post-civil rights political rhetoric. Garland-Thomson's argument that Lorde claims physical difference as "exceptional," while crucial to the project of depathologizing disability, has been criticized for not doing justice to Lorde's work (see Chinn), but I also find the argument about "self-exhibition" (Garland-Thomson, *Extraordinary Bodies* 133) closer to more individualistic narratives which both *Zami* and Lorde's cancer journals question by paying attention to community-based activism and identifications. It is these aspects which I am interested in exploring in this essay, together with a consideration of Lorde's more personal response to illness, while reflecting on the complex ways in which her experiences with cancer fit into the larger tapestry of her work as a black woman.

I.

> Growing up Fat Black Female and almost blind in America requires so much surviving that you have to learn from it or die. [S]urvival is only part of the task. The other part is teaching. I have been in training for a long time.
>
> (*The Cancer Journals* 30)[1]

In her "biomythography" *Zami*, Lorde writes that she grew up with "no words for racism" (81). However, she manages to communicate its devastating effects through the eyes of a child who tries to understand why she is not treated like the other children at school and through a language that returns to the ways the body registers marginalisation and violence. In these early sections of *Zami*, disability and race operate together in an intricate system. In the initial chapters Lorde describes herself as "legally blind" and mentions that "the doctors at the clinic had clipped the little membrane under my tongue so that I was no longer tongue-tied" (23). Such details are neither purely literal nor entirely figurative, and therefore help us see how disability and race mutually constitute each other. Elizabeth Alexander is right to note that the emphasis on legality in "legally blind" calls up the ironies of legal and extralegal categories in African-American life" (701). Building upon a chronological coincidence to elaborate the homologous structures of power that obtain in the public and private spheres, *Zami* often includes historical events of significance that determine the protagonist's movements across homes. In most cases, these refer to the passing or the enforcement of laws which illustrate either Lorde's distrust of the American legal system, as with the Rosenbergs' struggle which becomes "synonymous with being able to live in this country [America] at all" (149) – Lorde leaves for Mexico after they are electrocuted – or a renewed faith in it, as in the case of Brown vs Board of Education passed by the United States Supreme Court in 1954, which "feels like a private promise, some message of vindication particular to me" (172). But, in this initial scene, the qualifier "legally," while not obscuring disability (Audre is literally semi-blind) evokes the ironies noted by Alexander, and, in this way, alerts us to the intersection of race and disability. In turn, the tongue-cutting incident literalises the violent entry into the symbolic, but Lorde also uses it to open up a broader discussion about silence, voice and who has the right to them. Dismissing the stereotype of the black as cognitively disabled, the standard interpretative frame of the time, Lorde notes: "I don't know if I didn't talk earlier because I didn't know how or if I didn't talk because I had nothing to say that I would be allowed to say without punishment" (22).

In her first school, the teacher divides the class into two groups: "the Fairies" and "the Brownies" and, as the narrator explains, "one was put into the Brownies if one misbehaved, or couldn't learn to read" (28). The names are supposed to be neutral but as the mature voice of the narrative notes, filtering the experience lived by the child, "In this day of heightened sensitivity to racism and color usage, I don't have to tell you which were the good students and which were the baddies" (27-28). The school provides an early platform to excel in upward mobility skills; the desired goal is to join the Fairies, in other words, to become white, which, here, becomes equated with smartness. Once more, the narrator gives "a tangible, corporeal image" (Alexander 702) of mobility being constrained for the "Brownies": "The thing that I remember best about being in the first grade was how uncomfortable it was, always having to leave room for my guardian angel on those tiny seats, and moving back and forth across the room from Brownies to Fairies and back again" (30).

The stereotype of non-white races as "evolutionary laggards" (Baynton 36), which was germane to the justification of slavery, resonates in Lorde's treatment by both her teachers and classmates at school. Sister Mary, Lorde's first grade teacher in the Catholic school she enrols, is supposed to be dedicated to the care of "the Colored and Indian children of america [sic]", but, as Lorde clarifies the notion of 'care,' "Caring for was not always caring about" (27). Audre's sentence "I like White Rose Salada Tea" (29), which uses collage (Audre clips words out from a newspaper ad for her sentence), is more elaborate and sophisticated than other students', or, as Lorde puts it, "was too much coming from a Brownie" (ibid.), which is why the teacher has doubts of the authenticity of its authorship and requests proof, in the form of a note, by Audre's mother. This scene has echoes of the famous case of eighteen-year-old slave Phillis Wheatley, whose poems were examined by a panel of Boston's most prominent citizens in order to establish whether they were indeed authentic. The conclusion, in both cases, is a happy one: "Triumphantly, I gathered up my books and moved back over to the Fairies" (30). It seems, here, that Lorde's younger self (unlike the older one, as we will see) seeks "assimilation" which could be partly explained by the fact that she still has no words for racism or, even, for racial difference, due to her parents' silence (in another scene in *Zami*, Audre announces to the horror of her sisters that if anybody asks her what she is, she is going to tell them that she is "white same as Mommy" [59]).[2]

But just as the verdict in Wheatley's case does not signal the end of slavery, discrimination continues for Audre who cannot simply be accepted as the same. In her second school, there is no moving back and forth across spaces, however deterministic or physically uncomfortable, but segregation and a complete lack of access; both institutional and physical. The scene with the school elections is particularly evocative. Sister Blanche announces that they are going to hold elections for two class presidents, one boy and one girl, and that the voting should be according to merit and effort and class spirit. The person, however, who ends up being elected is the prettiest girl in class with her "blonde curls"

(61) and, no need to mention, the standards of prettiness are those of the white society. Audre, who is described indulging in fantasies of winning and of breaking the news to her mother, cannot comprehend the reason why she is not elected: "How could this have happened? I was the smartest girl in the class […]. It was as simple as that. But something was escaping me. Something was terribly wrong. It wasn't fair" (63).

Lorde's lack of language about racism while growing up, expressed through her constant state of confusion, always returns to the body: "What was it that kept people from inviting me to their houses, their parties, their summer homes for a weekend? Did their mothers caution them about never trusting outsiders? But they visited each other. […] There was something here that I was missing" (82). In this case, physical access is denied. Audre's classmates make fun of her braids and leave notes at her desk that she "stinks" (60). Erving Goffman's "stigma" theory and Mary Douglas's concept of "dirt" are useful when examining such constructions of the non-normative body, since they also address race, and they have been extended by disability studies theorists (an example is Rosemarie Garland-Thomson's study *Extraordinary Bodies*). It is perhaps not accidental that while being at school, one of the non-black people Lorde associates with is Alvin; a boy described as wearing dirty clothes and smelling badly, and who, later, dies of tuberculosis (28). Though Audre is initially repelled by the boy, she notes that they manage to work out a system of mutual help which complements their "deficiencies" (Alvin cannot read words while Audre cannot recognise numbers).

Disability is not only racialised but race also signifies almost as a disability as it denies or regulates access to certain spaces. I make this suggestion with caution as I do not wish to fall into the simplistic generalisation that "To be black is like being disabled" or that "To be disabled is like being black," which conflates race with disability. Still, race can be metaphorized as disability here; just as Audre has no access to her classmates' parties and other gatherings, in Jim Crow America, race becomes a "performance" of disability as African-Americans are denied admission to virtually all white-only establishments. Lorde writes about her rude awakening when a white waitress in Washington D.C. refuses to serve her family ice cream in the parlour because they are black.

> The waitress was white and the counter was white and the ice cream I
> never ate in Washington D.C. that summer I left childhood was white and
> the white heat and the white pavement and the white stone monuments of

my first Washington summer made me sick to my stomach for the whole rest of that trip and it wasn't much of a graduation present after all. (71)

Like Fanon, who feels "nausea" (112), in other words has a physical response to racism, in the well-known incident described in *Black Skin, White Masks* ("Mama, see the Negro! I am frightened!"), Lorde "in-corporates the intellectual and physical aspects of her life, reminding the reader that the metaphysical resides in a physical space, the body" (Alexander 697). Abstract things are physical before they "metabolise" to become metaphysical (ibid. 709), which once more establishes the body as the boundary between the subject and the world. Lorde, as we will see, later rewrites this scene of incorporation in terms that suggest that even the worst sustenance can be nourishing and empowering. As she writes in *Sister Outsider*,

> one of the most basic Black survival skills is the ability to change, to metabolise experience, good or ill, into something that is useful, lasting, effective. Four hundred years of survival as an endangered species has taught most of us that if we intend to live, we had better become fast learners. (182)

Through practices of social segregation as the above, black Americans are presented as both figuratively and literally disabled in the nation. As Lorde writes about the trip to Washington, what starts as a Fourth of July trip to "the fabled and famous capital of *our* country" (68, my emphasis) ends with a realisation of the "travesty such a celebration was for Black people in *this* country" (69, my emphasis). If social practices of segregation police movement and translate race into a form of disability in America, Lorde posits Mexico as "the *accessible* land of color and fantasy and delight, full of sun, music and song" (147, my emphasis). Accessible, here obviously means that it is relatively easy for a North American person to cross the border – Lorde writes that she "could always walk there" (ibid.) – but, if approached figuratively, it can be suggested that Mexico, however Orientalizing the effect of its description may seem, does not provide merely literal or physical access. The narrator sees for the first time her colour being "reflected upon the streets in such great numbers" (156). As she confesses, this "was an affirmation for me that was brand-new and very exciting. I had never felt visible before, nor even known I lacked it" (ibid.). Sarah E. Chinn writes that "the gaze works either affirmatively, to render an other (whether disabled, black, gay) hypervisible, or negatively, to ignore the other, as though she were invisible" (186-87). Mexico appears as a utopian land for people of colour in that they are neither made to feel invisible nor hypervisible. Finding the right balance between excessive visibility and invisibility is not problematic, and Lorde welcomes the attention she receives in Mexico feeling "bold and adventurous and special" (154).

II.

> Yet while I was watching [*Terms of Endearment*], involved in the situation of a young mother dying of breast cancer, I was also very aware of that standard of living, taken for granted in the film, that made the expression of her tragedy possible. Her mother's maid and the manicured garden, the unremarked but very tangible money so evident through its effects. Daughter's philandering husband is an unsuccessful English professor, but they still live in a white-shingled house with trees, not in some rack-ass tenement on the Lower East side or in Harlem for which they pay too much rent. Her private room in Lincoln Memorial Hospital has her mama's Renoir on the wall. There are never any Black people at all visible in that hospital in Lincoln, Nebraska, not even in the background. Now this may not make her death scenes any less touching, but it did strengthen my resolve to talk about my experiences with cancer as a Black woman.
>
> ("Burst of Light" 331)

In *Warrior Poet: A Biography of Audre Lorde*, Alexis De Veaux suggests that "the impact of cancer performed a transfiguration not only of Lorde's physicality but of her personality, creativity, and social activism" (xii).[3] In the following sections, I will focus on the impact her illness had on all these aspects of Lorde's life. Lorde's adamant refusal of prosthesis in *The Cancer Journals* has created a powerful narrative of feminist and patient resistance; in dismissing private suffering and reclaiming the capacity to tell one's own story, Lorde refuses to surrender to the authority of the medical narrative and to the construction of the female as "decoration and externally defined sex object" (47). Even though she looks "strange and uneven and peculiar" without a prosthesis (33), she asserts: "[E]ither I would love my body one-breasted now, or remain forever alien to myself" (33). Not unlike Jo Spence, a photographer working around the same time in Britain, Lorde offers a unique insight of the power dynamics of the doctor/patient relationship and the role of the healthcare institution, as well as of women's collusion in their "infantilization" as patients. Like other feminists of her time, she breaks the silence about women's issues, and demonstrates how the personal is political. Her MLA speech in 1977 is appropriately entitled "The Transformation of Silence into Language and Action," and Lorde uses her own experience of cancer to illustrate how a personal struggle can become politically useful.

However, Lorde does more than voice what is hidden, shameful, and unspoken. Her critique of prosthesis exposes regulatory processes of normalisation which position women vis-à-vis a universal or unmarked body ideal. The demand for "a normal body," on which the choice of prosthesis is based, pays no attention to women's own perception of who they are. Lorde writes that "where normal means the right color, shape, size or number of breasts, a woman's perception of her own body and her strengths that come from that perception are discouraged, trivialized and ignored" (51). Positing prosthesis as a technique of "disciplinary normalization" of the female body, to echo Foucault, Lorde theorises "new constructions of embodiment" (Shildrick and Price 439) which do not incorporate difference through a façade of sameness. Lorde affirms that there are various sizes and shapes of being a woman which do not fit what, in *Sister Outsider*, she calls "the mythic dehumanizing norm" (186). This applies to issues of racial and sexual difference, but also to disability.

Even though Lorde writes in her introduction to the *Cancer Journals* that "there is a commonality of isolation and painful reassessment which is shared by all women with breast cancer" (4), her account importantly reveals that what "makes an experience real is its particulars" (Frank, *At the Will of the Body* 46). As Frank writes, "One person's anger or grief may differ so much from another's that calling them by a common name only obscures what is actually going on for each" (ibid.). A scene which demonstrates how the questions one wants to ask about her life remain unspeakable or even unthinkable within mainstream understandings of a disease like breast cancer is when Lorde receives a visitor at the hospital from Reach of Recovery after her mastectomy. While the woman talks about the advantages of prosthesis for all women, Lorde "look[s] away," thinking:

'I wonder if there are any black lesbian feminists in Reach for Recovery?' I ached to talk to women about the experience I had just been through. [...] But I needed to talk with women who shared at least some of my major concerns and beliefs and visions, who shared at least some of my language. And this lady, admirable though she might be, did not. (32)

When the woman tells Lorde that prosthesis "doesn't really interfere with your love life," presuming that Lorde is heterosexual, and continues talking about her husband, Lorde is thinking: "What is it like to be making love to a woman and have only one breast brushing against her" (ibid.). Lorde's thoughts (not voiced at the time the incident took place) speak volumes about how some people may experience illness or disability as interwoven with other conflicts and challenges.

Moreover, the woman's statement that with prosthesis "you'll never know the difference" (31) seems immediately absurd: Lorde tries it on standing in front of a mirror and observes that "it perched on my chest askew, awkwardly inert and lifeless, and having nothing to do with any me I could conceive of." "Besides," she notes, seemingly in passing, "it was the wrong color [pink], and I looked grotesquely pale through the cloth of my bra" (33).[4] Racial difference is here rendered invisible and it seems as if it has nothing to do with the universal experience of illness. In light of this, the title of the second chapter of *The Cancer Journals*, namely, "Breast Cancer: A Black Lesbian Feminist Experience" is not accidental or misleading. Nor would it be fair to dismiss Lorde's vision of an army of single-breasted "amazons" without second thought for being too romantic or old-fashioned. As Frank explains, "It is a potent metaphor for her new identity, the one-breasted woman warrior, complete with third-world location and lesbian connotations" (*The Wounded Storyteller* 129).[5]

Lorde's account of illness is interspersed with traces which constantly remind her readers that the body whose story is told is not unmarked. Looking at the surgical area, Lorde writes that she "saw her same soft *brown* skin" (33) and when she tries writing, finding the pain impossible, she notes that "What seems impossible is made real/tangible by the physical form of my *brown* arm moving across the page; not that my arm cannot do it, but that something holds it away" (40, my emphasis). Just as Lorde chooses the amazons as her model, because they are more relevant to her own experience, it can be understood why lyrics by Jamaican musician Bob Marley recur in the text, passing a more hopeful message than the one communicated by the woman from Reach of Recovery, or why Lorde appeals to the goddesses and gods of the Yoruba peoples and to African mythology. In some cases, Lorde risks even alienating her white female readers, who may identify with her on the basis of a common female illness, as when we read that "if one *Black* woman I do not know gains hope and strength from my story, then it has been worth the difficulty of telling" (332, my emphasis). Statements like the above seem to contradict Lorde's suggestion in her introduction that she is writing for all women, but serve, nevertheless, an important purpose.

In "Burst of Light," Lorde returns to the problem of women's infantilization by doctors, but she also reveals how such practices converge with racism:

> When I told [my doctor] I was having second thoughts about a liver biopsy, he glanced at my chart. Racism and Sexism joined hands across his table as he saw I taught at a university. 'Well, you look like an intelligent girl,' he said, staring at my breast all the time he was speaking. (319)

Here, race, disability, and gender literally "intersect," as is suggested by the image of "joining hands" and the doctor's simultaneous gaze (or, rather, stare).[6] In an interview, Alexander sees Lorde's decision not to follow the doctor's prescriptive path at this stage as a metaphor for black struggle:

> I can't even imagine being Audre Lorde and the doctors saying you will die if we don't cut your liver out. And one after the other and saying you know, I'm going to – you know, there are other ways of thinking in the world and I'm going to go around the world. And I'm going to learn how other people have dealt with this. I think that's a metaphor, too. That's a metaphor. You know, what would it mean – what would it mean if all of the black women throughout history and to this day had swallowed and acted upon that which was said about us? We wouldn't survive. I don't think we would. (Qtd. in Jones 12)

Lorde does not see her act of caring for her body as a form of "self-indulgence" (332), and elsewhere she writes that "every woman has a militant responsibility to involve herself actively with her own health" (58). In *Sisters of the Yam: Black Women and Self-Recovery*, which was inspired by Lorde's *Sister Outsider*, bell hooks dispels the myth that black bodies do not need care. She traces a history of servitude, which has made black women internalise the assumption that their bodies do not matter (88-89). Lorde, of course, acknowledges that she leads "a privileged life or else [she] would be dead by now" (322).[7] The epigraph of this section shows her sensitivity to the fact that not all women can cope with illness in the same way. There are many instances in *The Cancer Journals*, but also elsewhere, where Lorde draws attention to the inequality of the disease. In "An Open Letter to Mary Daly," where she critiques the use of exclusively western myths for feminist empowerment in Daly's book *Gyn/Ecology*, she writes:

> Surely you know that for nonwhite women in this country, there is an 80 percent fatality rate from breast cancer; three times the number of unnecessary eventrations, hysterectomies and sterilizations as for white women; three times as many chances of being raped, murdered, assaulted as exist for white women. These are statistical facts, not coincidences nor paranoid fantasies. (122)[8]

At the same time, however, with her recognition that she is more privileged than other black women with cancer, Lorde not only corrects the tendency to see disabled communities as monolithic (through the lack of attention to racial or ethnic diversity), but also stresses the need to pay attention to differences within black communities themselves (such as, in this case, those of class).

Lorde's position towards prosthesis cannot be seen outside such particulars, as her race and lesbianism, which shape her own experience of breast cancer. This is why I am sceptical about Diane Price Herndl's conclusion in her theoretical-confessional essay "Reconstructing the Posthuman Feminist Body Twenty Years after Audre Lorde's *Cancer Journals*" that Lorde's position is simply grounded in "an *earlier* understanding of self that may not be comfortable for many postmodern feminists," and that "her refusal to wear a prosthesis was an open avowal of something that had remained hidden" (150). Lorde, indeed, inhabits a different historical moment, and I agree that she has helped destigmatize the disease and increase the visibility of women suffering from it. She also exposes hierarchical categories of thinking about disability itself, as when she criticises society for seeing a male politician with an eye patch appearing on television as a warrior or as a casualty in a heroic war,[9] while her scar is seen as a source of shame that has to be covered. However, Herndl's argument that "in the twenty years since Lorde wrote *The Cancer Journals*, *we* have come to think about bodies differently" (153, my emphasis) raises the question to whom "we" refers and which women would be likely to invoke the postmodern sense of alienation and the sophisticated theories that Herndl draws upon for her self-justification. The expensive methods of breast reconstruction discussed in the essay are not of course readily available to all women given the inequalities that continue to surround prevention, detection, and treatment of breast cancer.

More importantly, Herndl's essay conveniently omits, perhaps in order to make her continuity with Lorde's "feminist choice" more convincing, how Lorde uses her critique in order to articulate other invisibilities, which cannot be separated from the politics of prosthesis; in other words, prosthesis becomes an important metaphor for Lorde. The prosthesis she tries on at the hospital cannot feel like Lorde's lost breast, and in this sense, Lorde is nostalgic for what Herndl calls "the pretechnological body," a more romantic conception of the self: "I want the old me, bad as before" (5). At the same time, however, Lorde embraces her "new and changed landscape" (34), and criticises the "regressive tie to the past," the feeling "of wanting to go back, of not wanting to persevere through this experience [of cancer and post-mastectomy] to whatever enlightenment might be at the core of it" (43). Nostalgia in this second sense becomes equated with complacency. It is interesting to observe how Lorde uses the word "cosmetic" and its derivatives outside the narrow context of breast cancer and reconstruction. In *Sister Outsider*, for instance, she writes: "The old patterns, no matter how clearly rearranged to imitate progress, still condemn us to *cosmetically* altered repetitions of the same old exchanges, the same old guilt, hatred, recrimination, lamentation and suspicion" (170, my emphasis).[10]

Elsewhere, her critique of prosthesis addresses lesbian identity and race while emphasising the importance of common struggle. Socially sanctioned prosthesis is merely "another way of keeping women with breast cancer silent and separate from each other" (10). As she clarifies this statement: "Surrounded by other women day by day, all of whom *appear* to have two breasts, it is very difficult sometimes to remember that I AM NOT ALONE" (48). Those whose disabilities are not visible are pressured to try to pass as "able-bodied." Prosthesis is part of what Robert McRuer calls a system of "compulsory able-bodiedness" (91), which works in a similar way to Rich's notion of "compulsory heterosexuality." In *Zami*, which was written after *The Cancer Journals*, Lorde shows the convergence of the two systems writing about the invisible but visible sisters who pass her in the street "unacknowledged and unadmitted" (58), referring to black lesbian women. These women for Lorde are forced to wear a "straight" prosthesis or mask to cover their lesbianism. Finally, in an interview where Lorde talks about employment discrimination against women having undergone mastectomies, prosthesis becomes the pretext to introduce the theme of "racial passing." For Lorde, both prosthesis and passing are the result of the pressure to assimilate:

> Women who say, ah, yes, but there's so much discrimination against me
> to begin with, I didn't even want to tell them I had breast cancer. I'd say it
> was plastic surgery. They're terrified that they would lose their jobs, that
> people's attitudes –. And I can really hear that. Except I know – and the
> reason why I know this is because I was born black and a woman in the
> United States of America – I know that the way to fight that stuff is not to
> pretend it didn't happen. I mean, that really is like saying the way to com-
> bat racism is to pretend you're white. (Qtd. in Schultz 139).[11]

Lorde does not problematize the parallel she is drawing in the above quotation,
and it may be suggested that her account ultimately privileges race in that she is
not specifically concerned here with describing how disability and race intertwine (it is as if she assumes able-bodiedness for people of color). Her point
serves mostly a rhetorical purpose, namely, to encourage people who are in
similar positions of disempowerment to turn silence into voice and action. This
becomes clear in another instance from *The Cancer Journals* where Lorde argues that "employment discrimination against post-mastectomy women can only
be fought in the open, with head-on attacks by strong and self-accepting women
who refuse to be relegated to an inferior position, or to cower in a corner because they have one breast" (52). To recall her amazon metaphor, which seems
to be a better example of the convergence of disability and race (but also of lesbianism), Lorde's vision of "an army of one-breasted women descend[ing] upon
Congress and demand[ing] that the use of carcinogenic, fat stored hormones in
beef-feed be outlawed" (10) is not quixotic but seeks to make a society "openly
face the result of its own insanities" (48).

III.

> There is no room around me in which to be still, to examine and explore
> what pain is mine alone – no device to separate my struggle within from
> my fury at the outside world's viciousness, the stupid brutal lack of con-
> sciousness or concern that passes for the way things are.
>
> *(The Cancer Journals* 6)

Undoubtedly, one of the reasons Lorde's *Cancer Journals* speaks so powerfully,
even more than twenty years after its publication, has to do with the fact that it
not only offers a personal account of loss and mourning, but also transforms it
into a form of public discourse and cultural critique. On reading a letter from a

doctor in a medical magazine "which said that no truly happy person ever gets cancer," Lorde wonders in *The Cancer Journals* whether she had "really been guilty of the crime of not being happy in this best of all possible infernos" (59). For a moment she hesitates: "Was I wrong to be working so hard against the oppressions afflicting women and Black people? Was I doing all this to merely avoid my first and greatest responsibility – to be happy?" (59-60) For Susan Sontag, psychological theories of illness start from a wish to assert the triumph of will power over disease, but end up stigmatising illness and "placing the blame on the ill: patients who are instructed that they have, unwittingly, caused their disease are also being made to feel that they have deserved it" (58). For Lorde, this "guilt trip" "does nothing to encourage the mobilization of our psychic defenses against the very real forms of death which surround us" (59). Lorde draws from a list of crimes perpetuated at the time, but, it takes perhaps only a few changes of places, dates, and numbers, to make this passage feel "contemporary":

> In this disastrous time when little girls are still being stitched shut between their legs, when victims of cancer are urged to court more cancer in order to be attractive to men, when 12 year old Black boys are shot down in the street at random by uniformed men who are cleared of any wrongdoing, when ancient and honorable citizens scavenge for food in garbage pails, and the growing answer to all this is media hype or surgical lobotomy; when daily gruesome murders of women from coast to coast no longer warrant mention in *The N.Y. Times*, when grants to teach retarded children are cut in favor of more billion dollar airplanes, when 900 people commit mass suicide rather than face life in America, and we are told it is the job of the poor to stem inflation; what depraved monster could possibly be always happy?
>
> The only really happy people I have ever met are those of us who work against these deaths with all our energy, recognizing the deep and fundamental unhappiness with which we are surrounded, at the same time as we fight to keep from being submerged by it. But if the achievement and maintenance of perfect happiness is the only secret of a physically healthy life in America, then it is a wonder that we are not all dying of a malignant society. (60)[12]

The discourse of "happiness" that Lorde scorns is used to caution the Americans about what they could become (in other words, ill) if they were to betray their fundamental obligation to be happy. This, Lorde associates with a "superficial" mentality of "looking on the bright side of things"; "an euphemism used for obscuring certain realities of life, the open consideration of which might prove threatening or dangerous to the status quo" (59). This insight is perhaps relevant today more than ever in light of "the tyranny of cheerfulness," in Samantha King's phrase (103), which sees any expression of anger by breast cancer victims as a kind of betrayal; the result being a gradual de-politicization of the disease as it becomes divorced from broader social struggles of which the fight against cancer is just one part.

Passages as the above, which deals with the question of happiness, exhibit a certain verbal activity discussed by Foucault in a series of lectures given at the University of California at Berkeley in 1983. I am referring to "parrhesia" (occurring in Greek texts from the Fifth Century BC to the Fifth Century AD), and broadly translated as "free speech."[13] In his seminar "Discourse and Truth," Foucault suggests that parrhesia "is linked to courage in the face of danger: it demands the courage to speak the truth in spite of some danger" because the parrhesiastes, that is, the person who exercises it, "recognizes truth-telling as a duty to improve or help other people and himself" (parrhesiastes is always male in ancient Greece). As Foucault notes, "in its extreme form, telling the truth takes place in the 'game' of life or death." The parrhesiastes speaks from a position of less power; the parrhesia "comes from 'below,' as it were, and is directed towards 'above.'" The following passage from "Burst of Light" seems to match such characteristics:

> I wonder what I may be risking as I become more and more committed to telling whatever truth comes across my eyes my tongue my pen – no matter how difficult – the world as I see it people as I feel them. And I wonder what I will have to pay someday for that privilege, and in whose coin? Will those forces which serve non-life in the name of power and profit kill me too, or merely dismember me in the eyes of whoever can use what I do? (271)[14]

Lorde's "free speech" is inseparable from what I will proceed to describe as a particular kind of "generosity," which, if we accept De Veaux's claim that cancer radically changed Lorde's life, also derives from the experience of illness.

Lorde negotiates a delicate balance in her approach to illness. She seeks a way to "integrate death into living, neither ignoring it nor giving in to it" (7). Garland-Thomson argues that "our collective cultural consciousness emphatically denies the knowledge of vulnerability, contingency, and mortality" ("Integrating Disability" 21). In *The Body Silent*, referring to American culture in particular, Robert Murphy contends that disability is approached as a form of betrayal of the Puritan ideal of continuous improvement. As he puts it, "We [disabled people] are subverters of an American Ideal, just as the poor are betrayers of the American Dream" (116-17). Like Garland-Thomson and Murphy, Lorde is interested in showing how bodily limits can be accommodated rather than eliminated without immobilizing the self: "Living with cancer has forced me to consciously jettison the myth of omnipotence, of believing or loosely asserting that I can do anything, along with any dangerous illusion of immortality" (335). But this does not signal defeat. As Lorde adds, "But in their place, another kind of power is growing, tempered and enduring, grounded within the realities of what I am in fact doing" (ibid.). Lorde sees her refusal to turn away from pain as a "particularly African" characteristic, which "is transposed into the best of African-American literature" (qtd. in Tate 96-97), and, while assessing what is the best way to deal with her illness, she thinks of "the African way of perceiving life as experience to be lived rather than problem to be solved" (321).

Substituting the myth of omnipotence for the new, tempered and enduring, power she discovers becomes a step towards self-knowledge but also towards an ethics of care, which emphasizes relationships and responsibilities to others. In Lorde's texts, this ethics is specifically a feminist one, and is also connected to lesbian sexuality.[15] Lorde adopts a collective naming in her biomythography, the name "*Zami*," which is "a Carriacou name for women who work together as friends and lovers" (255).[16] The prologue of this text begins with the question "to whom do I owe the symbols of my survival" (3), and continues with an acknowledgement of names. Similarly, in *The Cancer Journals* Lorde recognises the help of a female network of friends and lovers: "To this day, sometimes, I feel like a corporate effort, the love and care and concern of so many women having been invested in me with such open-heartedness" (21). In "Burst of Light," she inserts herself in a maternal lineage which fills her with energy to fight cancer: "I hear the water's song, feel the tides within the fluids of my body, hear the sea echoing my mothers' voices of survival from Elmina to Grenville to Harlem. I hear them resounding inside me from swish to boom – from the dark of the moon to fullness" (305). The epilogue of *Zami* once more lists the women whom Lorde calls her "journeywoman pieces" (5), not only mythical figures like Afrekete but also "earthly" women such as Eudora with her scarred breast, fat DeLois, and moribund Louise Briscoe with "her huge bloated body" (4). In "Burst of Light," as we will see, this female network expands to embrace black women from all over the world.

Lorde's statement that there is "no device to separate my struggle within from my fury at the outside world's viciousness" in the epigraph of this section is reflected in the ways she visualises cancer. As she asserts, visualising the process of cancer "*inside my body in political images is not a quixotic dream*" (334, emphasis in the original). Because cancer has "an anonymous face," it is sometimes easier "to turn away from the particular experience into the sadness of loss" (334), and Lorde refuses, in what seems contrary to Sontag's view, to see cancer "as if it were just a disease" "without 'meaning'" (100). Given that Lorde seeks to explore how her experiences with cancer fit into the larger tapestry of her work as a black woman, cancer becomes "another face of that continuing battle for self-determination and survival that Black women fight daily, often in triumph" (269), and therefore provides her "with important prototypes for doing battle in all other areas of [her] life" (321). Unlike Sontag who wishes "to calm the imagination" (99) with her study *Illness as Metaphor*, Lorde's journals, interviews, and poems seem to incite it. Her poem "Never to Dream of Spiders," for instance, was written after the doctor tells her she has cancer of the liver, and Lorde compares the feeling in her body to a powerful image from the civil rights era, which, as Lorde explains in an interview, "lasted for me all of these years"; the phrase "when they turned the hoses upon me" in the poem refers to protests in Birmingham in which children were treated brutally after fire hoses were turned on them. Lorde describes an image that has been imprinted in her eyes: a girl in a black skirt and little white blouse holding hands with a young man, running, before the hoses literally bend her in half and sweep her across the street (qtd. in Abod 162-63).

In "A Burst of Light," the battle going on in Lorde's body merges with particular political campaigns all over the world. As she writes, cancer "at times takes on the face and shape of my most implacable enemies, those I fight and resist most fiercely" (334), such as racism, heterosexism, apartheid (321), and America's imperial interventions into the affairs of other countries and peoples.[17] Each battle for Lorde generates energies which are useful in others: "It takes all of my selves, working together, to effectively focus attention and action against the holocaust progressing in South Africa and the South Bronx and Black Schools across this nation, not to speak of the streets. It takes all of my selves working together to fight this death inside me" (308). Here, Lorde moves from settings of death all over the world to the death inside her. It is hard to pin down what the second sentence refers to: whether "inside" refers to her body and to cancer or whether it points to the ways she has incorporated the violence around her which has metabolised into cancer. As with her poetry, which keeps the reader suspended and challenges the pressure of sentence closure, one phrase here is able to mean differently depending on the words with which it makes contact, the words that precede and the words that follow (Avi-Ram 206).[18]

IV.

Construction

[…]

In Cancer

The most fertile of skysigns

I shall build a house

That will stand forever.

(Lorde, *The Collected Poems* 462)

I have done good work. There is a hell of a lot more I have to do. And sitting here tonight in this lovely green park in Berlin, dusk approaching and the walking willows leaning over the edge of the pool caressing each other's fingers, birds birds birds singing under and over the frogs, and the smell of new-mown grass enveloping my sad pen, I feel I still have enough moxie to do it all, on whatever terms I'm dealt, timely or not. Enough moxie to chew the whole world up and spit it out in bite-sized pieces, useful and warm and wet and delectable because they came out of my mouth.

("Burst of Light" 279)

In *Illness as Metaphor*, Sontag contends that "as long as so much militaristic hyperbole attaches to the description and treatment of cancer, it is a particularly unapt metaphor for the peaceloving" (86). War imagery is extensively used in *The Cancer Journals* and "Burst of Light," but the metaphor of the warrior does not preclude the idea of "constructing" a better world. It is primarily meant to counter "passive suffering" (59). Similarly, cancer conjures images of destruction and amputation, but Lorde also reconfigures it as "a fertile skysign" in which she will "build a house that will stand forever" in her poem "Construction" from her 1993 collection *The Marvelous Arithmetics of Distance* (see epigraph of this section). Construction is as potent a metaphor for Lorde as is the idea of "battle"; towards the end of "Burst of Light" Lorde alludes to "*building* a strong and elegant pathway toward transition" (335, my emphasis). "Building" becomes possible not only through individual work but also through determined efforts to work together across differences "for a livable future" (289). Peace is an important project here, but, of course, Lorde defines it carefully, just as she distinguishes between a "superficial" mentality of "looking on the bright side of things" and the happiness of those people who can mobilise their energies against the unhappiness that surrounds them. The following passage from "Burst of Light" is worth quoting at length:

> For me as an African-American woman writer, sisterhood and survival means it's not enough to say I believe in peace when my sister's children are dying in the streets of Soweto and New Caledonia in the South Pacific. Closer to home, what are we as Black women saying to our sons and our nephews and our students as they are, even now, being herded into the military and unemployment and despair, someday to become meat in the battles to occupy the lands of other people of Color? [...] What is our real work as Black women writers of the Diaspora? Our responsibilities to other Black women and their children across this globe we share [...]. Sitting with Black women all over the earth has made me think a great deal about what it means to be indigenous, and what my relationship as a Black woman in North America is to the land-rights struggles of the indigenous peoples to this land, to Native American Indian women, and how we can translate that consciousness into a new level of working together. In other words, how can we use each other's differences in our common battles for a livable future? (288-89)

"A Burst of Light," which consists of journal excerpts kept during the first three years of living with cancer of the liver, has sections as the above which stress Lorde's increasing interest in working with black diasporic women in Europe and around the world. For instance, while in Berlin, conducting a creative writing course and receiving alternative treatment for cancer, Lorde "discovers" and connects to the Afro-German women: "Who are they, the German women of the Diaspora? [...] What can we learn from our connected differences that will be useful to both, Afro-German and Afro-American?" (276) What "A Burst of Light" highlights is the need to forge more connections, to continue the dialogue, "to stretch as far as I can go" (335). Discovering "the marvelous arithmetics of distance," in these three years covered by the entries of "Burst of Light," Lorde travels to places like Berlin, Zürich, London, Holland, the South of France, the Caribbean, and Australia. Working together in transnational networks struggling for a joint future becomes crucial, both therapeutically and politically:

> We all have to die at least once. Making that death useful would be winning for me [...]. Just writing those words down snaps everything I want to do into a neon clarity. The European trip and the Afro-German women, the Sister Outsider collective in Holland, Gloria's great idea of starting an organization that can be a connection between us and South African women. For the first time I really feel that my writing has a substance and stature that will survive me. (279)

In his study *The Renewal of Generosity*, Arthur Frank writes: "When people get sick, they want to get well. Getting well may be all some ever want. But some whose world is taken apart by sickness want the world they put back together to be different. They feel blessed to be alive and they want to return this generosity" (55). Lorde is determined to resist giving herself over "like a sacrificial offering to the furious single-minded concentration upon cure that leaves no room to examine what living and fighting on a physical front can mean" (333). Frank's phrase "blessed to be alive" acquires new connotations in the context of a long struggle for survival: Lorde, like Morrison, and so many other writers, stresses the "miracle" of survival for black people: "For to survive in the mouth of this dragon we call America we have had to learn this first and most vital lesson – that we were never meant to survive" (14). The suggestion here is that both cancer victims and blacks "were never meant to survive." This dangerous position, however, opens up new responsibilities:

> Because the machine will try to grind you into dust anyway, whether or not we speak. We can sit in our corners mute forever while our sisters and our selves are wasted, while our children are distorted and destroyed, while our earth is poisoned, we can sit in our safe corners mute as bottles, and we still will be no less afraid. (14)

In "Burst of Light," Lorde reworks this idea, as she often does in her work.[19] She explains that there is a "terrible clarity that comes from living with cancer that can be empowering" if one does not turn aside from it: "What more can they do to me? My time is limited, and this is so for each one of us. So how will the opposition reward me for my silences?" (324) This realization becomes, however, an occasion for further "generosity," in Frank's sense of "expanding the scope of moral [and political] participation for the ill and disabled" (*Renewal* 60). Opening further the connections between the personal and the public/political made in *The Cancer Journals*, Lorde reflects on her responsibilities as an African American woman towards black women across the globe, fears for the world their children will inherit (285), and does not stop working for the vision of how she wants "this earth to be for the people who come after me" (324), thus continuing to live life in the only way that feels right. This is a highly moral and political stance.

A sense of limited time does not prevent Lorde from keeping "impossible demands clearly in view" (Frank, *Renewal* 58) and for working "for what has not yet been" (333): "I use the energy of dreams that are now impossible, not totally believing in them nor their power to become real, but recognizing them as templates for a future within which my labors can play a part" (323). Her powerful image of incorporation, when she says that she has "enough moxie to chew the whole world up and spit it out in bite-sized pieces, useful and warm and wet and delectable because they came out of my mouth" (see epigraph of this section), gives flesh and blood to what Frank describes as wanting "the world they put back together to be different" in his account of those who use their illness to renew generosity. It is worth noting that the theme of incorporation is also used in *Zami*, but, there, incorporation is literal: While working at a factory, which hires unskilled people and exposes them to radiation, Audre chews and spits out the X-ray crystals she has to count "with her strong teeth" flushing "the little shards of rock down the commode" in order to make more money by tricking her exploitative employers (146). The new image of Lorde spitting the world out "in bite-sized pieces" is a creative, not a destructive one, and confirms the suggestion, already mentioned, that "one of the most basic Black survival skills is the ability to change, to metabolise experience, good or ill, into something that is useful, lasting, effective." The notion of metabolism reappears in another well-cited passage, from which "Burst of Light" has also taken its name:

> This is no longer a time of waiting. It is a time for the real work's urgencies. It is a time enhanced by an iron reclamation of what I call the burst

of light – that inescapable knowledge, in the bone of my own physical limitation. Metabolized and integrated into the fabric of my days. (325)

As the physical transforms into metaphysical, the body, as the passage suggests,
functions once more as a means of knowing the self, but also as a means of
working together for change.

The word "work" recurs in "Burst of Light," and the phrase "I have done
good work" (279) functions almost like a refrain (see also epigraph of this section). Lorde stresses the militant responsibility to work for all those things that
"have not yet been," just as in "The Transformation of Silence into Language
and Action" she had challenged her audience to do the same:

> Perhaps, for some of you here today, I am the face of one of your fears.
> Because I am a woman, because I am black, because I am lesbian, be-
> cause I am myself, a black woman warrior poet *doing my work, come to
> ask you, are you doing yours?*" (13, my emphasis)

Unlike Lorde who plants what she needs to harvest later on her own, her readers
are privileged in that though she leaves them with the tantalizing question "are
you doing yours," she does so after having provided useful templates for battling
despair "born of fear and anger and powerlessness" (10). The following quotation, then, can be taken not only as referring to Lorde, who, while re-reading *The
Cancer Journals* feels as if she has found a crystal that has been buried at the
bottom of a mine, waiting to be discovered, but more importantly, to her readers;
for, it is we who have the power to return this generosity making her feel one
more time that her writing "has a substance and stature" that has indeed survived
her and will continue to do so:

> This is why the work is so important. Its power doesn't lie in the me that
> lives in the words so much as in the heart's blood pumping behind the eye
> that is reading, the muscle behind the desire that is sparked by the word –
> hope as a living state that propels us, open-eyed and fearful, into all the
> battles of our lives. And some of those battles we do not win.
>   But some of them we do. (293)

[1] All page numbers from *The Cancer Journals*, "Burst of Light," and *Sister Outsider* refer to *The Audre Lorde Compendium* edition.

[2] The skin of Lorde's mother is lighter (compared to her children) and she can pass as white, or, at least, as a Latina woman, as we find out in *Zami*.

[3] De Veaux divides the biography into two main sections: before, and after Lorde becomes diagnosed with cancer for the first time, and she call these "Lorde's two lives" (xi).

[4] There is a similar scene in *Zami* in which Audre resists buying nylon stockings, despite Ginger's (Lorde's lover and work colleague in Stamford) insistence, as she cannot stand "the bleached out color that the so-called neutral shade of all cheap nylons gave [her] legs" (132).

[5] A note in *The Cancer Journals* explains that the Amazons of Dahomey have their right breasts cut off to make themselves more effective archers (25).

[6] In *Extraordinary Bodies*, Rosemarie Garland-Thomson writes that "if the male gaze makes the normative female a sexual spectacle, then the stare sculpts the female subject into a grotesque spectacle" (26).

[7] In Lorde's biography, De Veaux writes that Lorde admits that she was more "well off" than other women and that she would have died sooner without support. Some of the trips she made to Europe for alternative, homeopathic treatment of cancer were indeed funded by her friends (353).

[8] This letter was written in 1979 when twelve Black women were murdered in the Boston area (119).

[9] See David Serlin's "The Other Arms Race" for hierarchies of value constructed within groups of differently-abled individuals. His essay specifically examines why veteran amputees constituted "a superior category on an unspoken continuum of disabled bodies" (54) in the aftermath of war and rise of the hyperpatriotic culture of the late 1940s.

[10] In her introduction to *Sister Outsider*, Nancy K. Bereano draws attention to the fact that although "*Sister Outsider* spans almost a decade of [Lorde's] work, nine of the fifteen pieces in this book were written in the years following Lorde's discovery that she might have/did have cancer" (72).

[11] The opening scene of the first chapter in *Zami* tells of Linda's (Lorde's mother) dismissal from her job as a maid when her employer realises that she is not "Spanish" but actually black (9).

[12] In "Audre Lorde: Reflections," a *Feminist Review* essay that brings together statements from several groups, among which a group of women who organised an evening to celebrate Audre's life and work in London, on the 18th of February 1993, Lorde's challenge of silence and invisibility is seen as defining contemporary tasks more sharply: "For in the context of the Europe of the 'New World Order': in which unification means fortification; in which there is an alarming increase in racist violence and murder; in which organized and systematic mass rape is carried out in the name of an 'ethnic cleansing' process reminiscent of another sinister period of European history, there is clear and present danger that silence and invisibility will yet again not protect us from horrors worse than our combined imaginations must muster" (7).

[13] I would like to thank Professor Arthur Frank for making the connection between Lorde and Foucault's reading of "parrhesia" at his speech "How Stories Make up People" that took place on the 15th of July 2008 in Edinburgh, and which was organised by The Centre for Research on Families and Relationships (CRFR), The University of Edinburgh.

[14] It is important to note that this passage appears in a journal entry in which Lorde recalls Martin Luther King's death.

[15] In the introduction to a special issue of *GLQ* on queer theory and disability studies, Robert McRuer and Abby L. Wilkerson argue that "one of the most important respects in which many queer narratives differ from the comparatively individualistic heterosexual narrative of illness is the attention they pay to community-based activism and identifications" (12). See Chinn for the ways in which lesbian sexuality becomes "a source of a new ethics of interconnection" (197) in *Zami*, and how this helps us rethink central disability tenets about difference and the gaze.

[16] For this ritual of naming Lorde draws on West African systems of naming (Kraft 149).

[17] See "Apartheid U.S.A." and "Grenada Revisited: An Interim Report" in *Burst of Light* and *Sister Outsider* respectively.

[18] See Avi-Ram on the *apo koinou* (in common) technique used by Lorde in her poetry. *Apo koinou* is a figure of speech in which "a single word or phrase is shared between two independent syntactic units" (Avi-Ram 191), recreating meaning.

[19] In "Burst of Light," Lorde explains how useful her previous work proves to be while going through cancer for a second time: "Reading *The Cancer Journals* in this place [Lukas Klinik, in Arlesheim, Switzerland] is like excavating words out of the earth, like turning up a crystal that has been buried at the bottom of a mine for a thousand years, waiting. [...] Like always, it feels like I plant what I will need to harvest, without consciousness" (293).

Works Cited

"Audre Lorde: Reflections." *Feminist Review* 45 (Autumn 1993): 4-8.

Abod, Jennifer. "Audre Lorde: A Radio Profile." 1987. *Conversations with Audre Lorde*. Ed. Joan Wylie Hall. Jackson: UP of Mississippi, 2004. 158-63.

Alexander, Elizabeth. "'Coming Out Blackened and Whole': Fragmentation and Reintegration in Audre Lorde's *Zami* and *The Cancer Journals*." *American Literary History* 6.4 (1994): 695-715.

Avi-Ram, Amitai F. "*Apo Koinou* in Lorde and the Moderns: Defining the Differences." *Callaloo* 9.1 (1986): 193-208.

Baynton, C. Douglas. "Disability and the Justification of Inequality in American
        History." *The New Disability History: American Perspectives*. Ed. Paul K.
        Longmore and Lauri Umansky. New York: New York UP, 2001. 33-57.

Bell, Chris. "Introducing White Disability Studies: A Modest Proposal." *The
        Disability Studies Reader*. 2nd ed. Ed. Lennard J. Davis. New York:
        Routledge, 2006. 275-82.

Bereano, K. Nancy. Introduction. *Sister Outsider: The Audre Lorde
        Compendium: Essays, Speeches and Journals*. London: Pandora, 1996.
        69-74.

Chinn, Sarah E. "Feeling Her Way: Audre Lorde and the Power of Touch."
        GLQ: A Journal of Lesbian and Gay Studies 9.1-2 (2003): 181-201.

De Veaux, Alexis. *Warrior Poet: A Biography of Audre Lorde*. New York:
        Norton, 2004.

Fanon, Frantz. *Black Skin, White Masks*. 1952. Trans. C. L. Markham. London:
        Pluto P, 1986.

Foucault, Michel. "Discourse and Truth: the Problematization of Parrhesia." *Six
        Lectures given by Michel Foucault at the University of California at
        Berkeley, Oct.-Nov. 1983*. 9 October 2008 <http://foucault.info/
        documents/parrhesia/>.

Frank, W. Arthur. *At the Will of the Body: Reflections on Illness*. New York:
        Mariner, 2002.

---. *The Renewal of Generosity: Illness, Medicine, and How to Live*. Chicago: U
        of Chicago P, 2004.

---. *The Wounded Storyteller: Body, Illness, and Ethics*. Chicago: U of Chicago
        P, 1997.

Garland-Thomson, Rosemarie. *Extraordinary Bodies: Figuring Physical
        Disability in American Culture and Literature*. New York: Columbia UP,
        1997.

---. "Integrating Disability, Transforming Feminist Theory." *NWSA Journal* 14.3
        (2002): 1-32.

Herndl, Diane Price. "Reconstructing the Posthuman Feminist Body Twenty
        Years after Audre Lorde's *Cancer Journals*." *Enabling the Humanities: A
        Sourcebook for Disability Studies in Language and Literature*. Ed.
        Rosemarie Garland-Thomson, Brenda Brueggeman, and Sharon Snyder.
        New York: MLA, 2002. 144-55.

hooks, bell. *Sisters of the Yam*: *Black Women and Self-Recovery*. Boston: South
    End P, 1993.

Jones, Meta DuEwa. Interview with Elizabeth Alexander. 9 Oct. 2008
    <http://www.elizabethalexander.net/Meta%20Jones%20Interview.pdf>.

King, Samantha. *Pink Ribbons, Inc: Breast Cancer and the Politics of
    Philanthropy*. London: U of Minnesota P, 2006.

Kraft, Marion. "The Creative Use of Difference." 1986. *Conversations with
    Audre Lorde*. Ed. Joan Wylie Hall. Jackson: UP of Mississippi, 2004.
    146-53.

Lorde, Audre. *The Audre Lorde Compendium: Essays, Speeches and Journals*.
    London: Pandora, 1996.

---. *The Collected Poems*. New York: Norton, 1997.

---. *Zami: A New Spelling of My Name*. London: Sheba Feminist, 1982.

McRuer, Robert. "Compulsory Able-Bodiedness and Queer/Disabled
    Existence." *Disability Studies: Enabling the Humanities*. Ed. Sharon L.
    Snyder, Brenda Jo Brueggemann, and Rosemarie Garland-Thomson. New
    York: MLA, 2002. 88-99.

McRuer, Robert, and Abby L. Wilkerson. "Cripping the (Queer) Nation." *GLQ:
    A Journal of Lesbian and Gay Studies* 9.1-2 (2003): 1-23.

Morris, David B. *Illness and Culture in the Postmodern Age*. Berkeley: U of
    California P, 1998.

Murphy, Robert F. *The Body Silent*. New York: Norton, 1990.

Perreault, Jeanne. *Writing Selves: Contemporary Feminist Autography*.
    Minneapolis: U of Minnesota P, 1995.

Rich, Adrienne. "Notes toward a Politics of Location." *Blood, Bread, and
    Poetry: Selected Prose, 1979-1985*. By Rich. London: Virago, 1987. 210-
    31.

Schultz, Dagmar "Audre Lorde on Her Cancer Illness." 1984. *Conversations
    with Audre Lorde*. Ed. Joan Wylie Hall. Jackson: UP of Mississippi, 2004.
    132-42.

Serlin, David. "The Other Arms Race." *The Disability Studies Reader*. 2nd ed.
    Ed. Lennard J. Davis. New York: Routledge, 2006. 49-65.

Shildrick, Margrit, and Janet Price. "Breaking the Boundaries of the Broken
    Body." *Feminist Theory and the Body: A Reader*. Edinburgh: Edinburgh
    UP, 1999. 432-44.

Smith, Sidonie. *Subjectivity, Identity, and the Body: Women's Autobiographical Practices in the Twentieth Century*. Bloomington and Indianapolis: Indiana UP, 1993.

Sontag, Susan. *Illness as Metaphor and AIDS and Its Metaphors*. London: Penguin, 1991.

Tate, Claudia. "Audre Lorde." 1982. *Conversations with Audre Lorde*. Ed. Joan Wylie Hall. Jackson: UP of Mississippi, 2004. 85-100.

Therí Alyce Pickens

Pinning Down the Phantasmagorical: Discourse of Pain and the Rupture of Post-Humanism in Evelyne Accad's *The Wounded Breast* and Audre Lorde's *The Cancer Journals*

When my copy of Evelyne Accad's *The Wounded Breast* arrived at my office, my colleagues gathered around the Amazon.com box with the usual zeal of bibliophiles, asking "What did you get?" as though the little brown box were a present from beloved relatives. While the gasp that erupted at the cover was not akin to that within a film, there was a palpable pause at the cover. I received the customary comment germane to most speechless academics: "Interesting." The cover is a photo of the author's nude chest, exposing her post-mastectomy bosom, radiation markings, and bald head. The author is reclined with one hand behind her head. In the next weeks, perhaps in an effort to shock and awe, I left the book on my desk, cover up. Many people picked it up and had the same reaction – a look, a pause, and an "interesting."

What became clear to me was that their reactions were very much indicative of the discourse surrounding pain itself. Specifically, my colleagues' (and my students') reactions to the text demonstrated a discomfort with the pain of other people. In the face of Accad's cover, there was a disintegration of language – much like Elaine Scarry describes in her text, *The Body in Pain*. Yet, there was something more to their remarks of "interesting." They succeeded, in a way peculiar to most of us academics, in giving voice to their own discomfort in a way that highlighted the discomfort itself. For me, the critical question about these texts surfaced at these moments: How do these authors describe their own pain? It wasn't just that language disintegrated, but that there was an articulation within the gaps of eloquence about pain. Their silences, their moments of stutter and rambling coagulate to pin down that which appears elusive, to pin down the phantasm of pain.

What I noticed about Evelyne Accad's text was that it was remarkably similar to one with which she has a great deal of intertextuality, Audre Lorde's

The Cancer Journals. Not only are these women discussing the same issues, approximately thirty years apart, but their concerns with illness, specifically cancer, and their bodies, particularly their gendered and racialized bodies, echoed one another. It is not that their pain, or their descriptions of pain are different from other women's cancer narratives, but their texts bind up their discussions of pain with their being women of color. That is, they understand their experiences with cancer in terms that are particularly racialized and gendered.

It is important to note that both Evelyne Accad and Audre Lorde garnered fame and, for some people, notoriety as thorns in the side of hegemonic discourse that sanctions the oppression and silencing of women of color by ignoring or dismissing the circumstances that govern their experience. Their academic work pierces this discourse, elucidating that the issues of women of color point to systemic racism and sexism: in short, society's failure to appropriately address the double bind in which women of color exist.[1] Their personal breast cancer narratives, *The Wounded Breast* and *The Cancer Journals* respectively, extend their scholarship by directing their gazes at the health care and pharmaceutical industries. Of central import to their discussions is the issue of pain: for Accad, this comes principally in the form of mental suffering and agonizing, while Lorde focuses primarily on pain within the body. In these narratives, pain is a starting point, a fact of the experience of breast cancer. Pain, then, because of the certainty with which they describe it, underscores the severity of the other socio-political issues they bring to the fore. Both texts mobilize discourses with which Accad and Lorde are already engaged – gender, sexuality, and race – but, undergird them with a discourse of pain, thwarting a master narrative of illness which would further ensconce all women, particularly women of color, in silence.

This discourse of pain is not simply a purging of their emotions. That is, the disintegration of language that they undergo advances beyond a personal narrative; they each make stringent critiques of the health care system, its treatment of cancer patients, and its lack of concern about issues women with cancer face. Though their critiques are far-reaching, I am much more concerned with their discussions of treatment, and breast prosthetics and reconstruction, as these discussions are particularly undergirded by their understanding of physical pain and emotional suffering. Each woman advocates activism as a way to combat the difficulties within the health care system: Evelyne Accad's activism is situated within her text; she uses her writing as a discursive activism that spans three continents, and cuts across class lines. Audre Lorde, in addition to using her text in this way, advocates a more overt form of political activism, including the protests by post-mastectomy women who do not wear prosthetics or have surgically reconstructed breasts. Their stances, because their discourse is underscored by an inability to articulate pain and a disintegration of language, posit a new understanding of the discourse of pain: namely, that their silence and lack of language is a starting point for useful political action.

I also contend that their insistence on activism, whether discursive or political, undercuts – because of its insistence on the body in pain – multiple points within post humanist-thought. Given that post-humanism questions the cogitating subject of Cartesian philosophy, asking whether that subject's act of being puts her at the center of the universe, it would seem that post-humanism would be especially apt for understanding a cancer narrative. After all, it would promote the constitution of a community of women who are intimately linked with machines, and underscore efforts to incorporate the patient into a medical team whose existence also incorporates that of machinery. For women of color especially, post-humanism would, in the eyes of Donna Haraway, cut across racial and class lines to reveal that we are all the same in our cyborg identities. As useful as Haraway's formulations may be, they obfuscate the lived experience of illness, and silence any possible political critique that arises from that corporeality. Accad and Lorde's narratives call attention to their bodies as disruptive of the cyborg ideal, suggesting that embodied experience need be ushered into the post-humanist discussion of political critique.

Before delving into either Accad's or Lorde's text, we first encounter the covers. What is most striking is that both covers challenge particular misconceptions vis-à-vis breast cancer and pain: namely, that it cannot be discussed explicitly and, in the case of Lorde, with humor. Accad's cover (see Fig. 5.1.) foregrounds the image of the post-mastectomy woman, reclined with a serious expression looking directly at the reader. The photo appears to be lit from above, with a pinkish light, mirroring that of a radiation therapy. Though the top of the book cuts across the woman's head, it is obvious that she is bald. The center of the photograph holds Accad's lack of breast – not with a medical gaze or a sexualized gaze – but, instead, with a gaze that is forthright. To borrow from Kenny Fries, Accad 'stares back.' Her forward stare, radiation marks, and missing breast emphasize the medical procedures that she has undergone and the aftermath of those procedures with regard to her body. In her photo, Accad does not lower her outward gaze, nor does she invite comfort. The photo appears to be a simple declarative statement: I am here. Lorde's cover makes a similar statement. On her cover is Audre Lorde, smiling and peering straight ahead, with her head tilted toward the title on the left. She looks out from a blank backdrop, which makes her smiling presence more insistent. As Elizabeth Alexander notes, this cover art foregrounds the fact of her existence (703): she is alive and talking.[2]

Fig. 5.1. Photo by Eva Enderlein, published in *The Wounded Breast: Intimate Journeys through Cancer*, Melbourne, Australia: Spinifex Press. Reproduced with permission from the publisher. www.spinifexpress.com.au.

But, the covers do not limit themselves to being declarative statements of presence. Because cancer is so often discussed through the metaphor of war, these images act as images of survivors and, indeed, the existence of the personal narrative buttresses the idea that this is a testimony of their experience. I do not intend to suggest that understanding cancer through a metaphor of war is unproblematic, especially given that the texts themselves go against such an understanding; however, the covers, as points of entry, rely somewhat on, if only to thwart, the dominant narratives created by photographs of war: sympathy for the survivors, treatment of subjects as victims, and the sensationalism of images. This is why Susan Sontag's *Regarding the Pain of Others* becomes apposite in reading these images as representations of an atrocity. In Sontag's text, she meditates on the depictions of war and their implications for how we understand war, sympathy and responsibility. Sontag argues that the images of war give primacy to the identity of the subjects and await a caption to explain them. Accad's cover image functions according to this understanding, giving primacy to female identity and the caption or, in this case, the book's author, title and subtitle – Evelyne Accad, *The Wounded Breast: Intimate Journeys through Cancer* – explains what the image is supposed to represent: a specific person, a wound, an intimate journey and cancer. Yet, this image also complicates female identity, identifying a missing breast as equally feminine to a present breast. That is, despite the sexualized narratives that require two (full) breasts as a prerequisite for womanhood, she is a woman whether she has one breast or two. Both the missing breast and the present breast support the notion that femininity and female identity are still present, despite the fact that the breasts in this photo are neither sexualized nor medicalized. In addition, the captions point to a plurality not present in the image itself. The plural noun 'journeys' repositions the woman as a representative. She becomes both an individual and an icon. Much like the war images in Sontag's text, this cover requires the engagement of images and ideas that exist outside the camera's scope to delineate a remodeled (excuse the pun) idea of femininity and the experience of cancer.

In *Regarding the Pain of Others*, Sontag problematizes these types of images because they are staged and rely primarily on identity. She rightly suggests that these images can be undercut by the narratives created about them and, certainly, taken out of context to mislead an audience. For Sontag, staged images create a mockery of the reality of suffering and undermine it as performative, a gesture that ultimately works to dismiss the responsibility of the viewer. Accad's cover image amplifies this theory, suggesting that an image can create its own context and narrative. In this case, the image where a subject owns her pain challenges the idea of the pain itself. First, the seriousness of the woman's expression, unflinching to be sure, implies that the portrait, the staged photo, is secondary to the reality of the missing breast. Here, the breast cannot be ignored or dismissed; it is precisely the presumed discomfort with the missing breast and the subject's forward stare that turn what would be a spectacle into a meditation on the reality of the missing breast. What appears to be performative – the large earrings, the hand at the back of the head – underscores the main subject of the photo: the focal point, the missing breast. In fact, the pose, the earrings and the nude present breast demonstrate an acceptance of the lack as a reality. As a result, the image invites engagement with itself and its subject matter. Nonetheless, the woman's ownership of (her presumed) pain does not invite pity;[3] instead, it prompts an interrogation of mastectomies and the experience of breast cancer.

Both Accad and Lorde's cover images point to a question central to Sontag's meditation on images: "What to do with such knowledge as photographs bring of faraway suffering? People are often unable to take in the sufferings of those close to them" (99). Sontag decides – interrogating a statement she made in *On Photography* (1977)[4] – that images continue to have power depending upon their context. Accad's cover relies on a reworking of the Venus de Milo image to create an impact. Likewise, Lorde's cover relies on the oft-used image of the laughing black woman to thwart the understanding of cancer. On Lorde's cover, the image insists on her presence, her happy presence. Nonetheless, this is not the smiling face of any stereotypical image of black women; she is not Jezebel or mammy. She is not scantily clad, nor is she taking care of anyone else in a domestic capacity. The blank background reinforces her presence by foregrounding it and also makes clearer the fact that her head tilts toward the title, *The Cancer Journals*. The pose and laughter add a sense of irony to the cover: the so-called victim of cancer (and implied victim of sexist and racist oppression) is not without a sense of humor. What becomes present in this interplay of categories – black, female, ill – is precisely its interplay and the fact that her subjectivity cannot be harnessed or completely explained by one identity category. This cover's power as an image lies precisely in the confusion elucidated by Sontag's question. What do we do with the suffering of this woman? In this way, Lorde's cover, as does Accad's, positions the text as the answer to these questions.

Sontag's answer to the same question relies on the viewer to be sensitive to the images before him; she understands the image and, therefore, the obligation of conscience to be more powerful when coupled with compassion that translates to action. As she says,

It is because a war, any war, doesn't seem as if it can be stopped that [sic] people become less responsive to the horrors. Compassion is an unstable emotion. It needs to be translated into action, or it withers. The question is what to do with the feelings that have been aroused, the knowledge that has been communicated. (101)

Accad and Lorde's texts attempt to translate images of cancer – both the concrete images of the covers and dominant images in the American imaginary – into specific issues that require action. For both authors, more than just the readers' sympathies and pity are at stake; there is political action to be done. That is to say, the texts work to harness sympathy and motivate to political action.

The structure of Accad's *The Wounded Breast* emphasizes the severity of cancer, not just the experience of the disease, but also the overabundance of it, the possibility of prevention and the systemic hindrances to a cure. *The Wounded Breast* traverses three continents and is flanked by a prologue and an epilogue written by the author. The multiplicity of places and people Accad encounters with cancer underscores the prevalence of cancer as minatory. Within her journal entries, Accad frequently laments the suffering of the people, particularly women, whom she loves and those with whom she has spoken. She also complains about the narratives that she hears but does not record; she talks about being bombarded with cancer stories. Her prologue and epilogue act as mirrors of the cover, forcing the text to reflect on its own subject and its author – both the missing breast(s) and the person(s) who've had them excised. Though the majority of the text is penned by Accad, her friends' marginalia riddle the text, punctuating, confirming, and complicating Accad's words. We experience not only Accad's thoughts but also those of her lover, Alban, her masseuse, Bettina, and her friends, Jane, Manicha, and Gilles. This chorus tends to support Accad most when she discusses her experiences with the health care system: the idea that her cancer was prompted by her doctor's error in prescribing Estrogen Replacement Therapy (ERT), the rude bed-side manner of other doctors, the possibility of healing through the mind, and the simultaneous guilt and duty these experiences place upon the patient, patient advocacy and patient rights, and, among other topics, the curative function of friendship. Their responses to Accad and to each other highlight the ways in which some experiences with cancer, namely, unnecessary radiation, carcinogenic ERT, and confusion on the part of patients, can be prevented. In her discussion of these experiences, Accad discusses the ways in which they affect women in particular; her critique relies on the female body. Accad also begins and ends each chapter with paragraph-length quotes from other memoirs and meditations on cancer, among them, Jeane Hyvrard's *Le cercan*, Sandra Steingraber's *Living Downstream: An Ecologist Looks at Cancer and the Environment*, and Gilles-Eric Séralini's *Le sursis de l'espèce humaine*. These quotes buttress Accad's journal entries by stating what she only hints at or briefly covers: the environmental causes of cancer, the officials that ignore toxic waste dumping, and the capitalist impulse preventing change in the status quo. In this manner, the suffering of Accad and others becomes needless and their anguish preventable.

The structure of Lorde's text also works to provoke political action. She nestles her journal entries within larger essays, mixing personal reflection with a critical eye. At times, this structure can be disorienting, but it does not verge into being desultory. In fact, her selected journal entries marshal her text just as much as her essays. The result of which is not just a meditation by an accomplished raconteur, but a self-reflexivity and introspection, which implies that, though Lorde has felt the effects of systems of oppression, she chooses to speak and act and, by extension, so can the reader. In other words, Lorde exposes the fallacies of the health care industry and how they affect women of color, and, because she reflects upon her position her subsequent choice, to write and to not "obscure [her] painful feelings surrounding mastectomy with a blanket of business-as-usual" (9), the text renders her political position the only natural outgrowth of reading this text. For example, in the chapter entitled, "Breast Cancer: Power vs. Prosthesis," Lorde enters her doctor's office, feeling confident of her style and flair without her breast only to be told by a nurse that Lorde's lack of prosthetic is "bad for the morale of the office" (59). This anecdote is flanked by critical contemplation of the understanding of a mastectomy as purely a cosmetic incident and a journal entry that buttresses Lorde's feelings with regard to the nurse's comment. The result of these multiple types of storytelling is a trifecta that fully demonstrates Lorde's point: Prosthetics mask the other issues surrounding breast cancer, most notably, but not limited to, a confrontation with one's own mortality, the criminalization of patients, dominant standards of beau-

ty (which do not include Lorde anyway), fear of recurrence, and the environmental factors that prompt cancer. The nurse's behavior demonstrates that she is
not only concerned with the less relevant topic of aesthetics, but also incapable
of providing the kind of psychological support needed by the patients for whom
she cares. So, when Lorde calls the prosthesis a "lie" (60), the text supports this
claim and clearly delineates what can be done about it. It makes Lorde's call for
a march of post-mastectomy women particularly apropos.

As the structure of both texts certainly elucidates the necessity of political
action and rally for environmental changes, *The Wounded Breast* and *The Cancer Journals* point to a familiar feminist discourse: namely, that the 'personal is
political.' More specifically, each text integrates homo-social bonds into the
healing process. Their friendships are not incidental or accidental; Accad and
Lorde rely on these friendships to process their experiences with breast cancer.
In their wrestling with these experiences and in particular their pain, their homo-
social bonds allow them to vacillate between fatigue and strength, feeling disen-
franchised and feeling empowered. Because of this vacillation, both women's
political action appears more necessary, more urgent. For instance, Accad narrates her difficulty with remaining inspired enough to fight for herself. Her
friends' marginalia provide her the space to be fatigued. She notes that this con-
tradicts the sentiments of Dr. Bernie Siegel, a medical professional who promotes people's ability to heal themselves and cultivate the inner peace that will
help them defeat cancer. Accad's text discusses this issue directly saying,

> I want to develop this inner peace and overcome the disease. At the same
> time, though, I find it revolting to always project responsibility on to the
> patient without talking about the political and environmental factors that
> are so obviously involved. (72)

Indeed, she wrestles with a desire for inner peace and the projection of responsibility onto herself throughout the text, often vacillating between the two and attempting to acknowledge the importance of both. Her wrestling is actually the
source of what she describes as her suffering. She does not understand how or
why one must undergo the loss of a mastectomy and the painful experiences of
chemotherapy and radiation. The text's polyvocality, made possible by her
friends' inserted comments, points to a reconciliation of having "inner peace"
and fighting the system. To give an example, Accad's discussion of her doctors'
poor bedside manner and the contradictions within the medical community (spe-

cifically those contradictions that result in poor patient care or uninformed consent) elicits remarks that support her political action and remind her to take care of herself. Fusing the two acknowledges the importance of the journal entries themselves, as acts that, to paraphrase Lorde, combat the silences that would be destructive (23).

In addition to the homo-social bonds of friendship, both Accad and Lorde tout the erotic as integral to healing as well. In so doing, they respond to the sterility of medical practice and, in opposition to the silence with which it is so often treated, voice the sexual concerns of breast cancer patients. Accad's discussion focuses on the transformation of intimacy and only briefly discusses the physical pain of penetration, saying that her vagina has shrunken. She laments the loss of a vibrant sexual life with her lover, Alban, and points out that "[her] intimate relationship with Alban was a real letdown that [she] needed to express" (106). Nonetheless, she also describes the happiness she feels when they are physically intimate, even if they cannot, as she says, "'take the elevator,' as [they] used to" (106). She and Alban remain sexual with one another and this love and intimacy become a source from which she draws strength. During her travels, she is anxious to return to him and longs to comfort him when he is diagnosed with prostate cancer. The intimate space of their sexual relationship positions sexuality and the erotic as antidotes to the silence surrounding sexuality and the rhetorical (and at times physical) sterilization of cancer patients by the medical establishment.

Lorde also privileges her relationship to the erotic as integral to her healing. She writes about her desire to masturbate in one of her journal entries saying, "one day when I found I could finally masturbate again, [I made] love to myself for hours at a time" (25). According to David Morris in his article "Unforgetting Asclepius: An Erotics of Illness," Lorde's candor about her need for auto-eroticism and other erotic experiences "enlists desire in aid of healing. It honors a tradition respectful of dream, ritual, and a bodily presence that cannot be reduced to manageable concepts or meanings" (434). Morris resituates sexuality into a discussion of the medical. His argument with respect to Lorde is that her erotic encounters disrupt the notion that she no longer has a sexual identity or sexual desires. I would add that her auto-erotic experiences in particular posit that she still has a sexual desire for herself and still views her body sexually after her mastectomy. The aforementioned journal entry appears in the chapter entitled "Breast Cancer: A Black Lesbian Feminist Experience." This narratological choice is especially apt given that erotic spaces complicate her identity in the face of a master narrative of illness that would totalize her experience and reduce her to being an asexual post-mastectomy woman. This title, much like the rest of the book, insists upon Lorde's identity as inclusive of many facets. Her text avoids reducing her to a woman who has had cancer, but ensures that her narrative about cancer evinces that she experienced cancer as a black, lesbian, feminist woman.

Thus far, I've discussed the ways in which Accad and Lorde use pain as an impetus for political activity and building alternative ways of healing. Their more direct discussions of pain tend to speak specifically to the master narratives governing cancer and cancer treatment. Because of this, Elaine Scarry's meditation on torture in *The Body in Pain* provides a lens to understanding both Accad and Lorde's larger critiques of the health care industry. In each narrative, the discussions of pain highlight the disintegration of language and the inability of others, particularly doctors and medical personnel, to view the post-mastectomy woman's pain as visible. Accad focuses on the "poison, cut and burn" (58) of chemotherapy, mastectomy, and radiation as treatment; whereas, Lorde engages in a discussion about phantom pains and other physical effects of the mastectomy. Scarry understands the collapse of language and the rendering of the tortured subject as invisible as two steps in a three-step process, the last of which is an insistence on the power of the regime that sanctions the torture. Both Accad's and Lorde's texts point toward an understanding of cancer and cancer treatment as torturous – indeed, Accad writes explicitly that it is torturous – and, highlight that these processes function to solidify the power of the medical establishment.

Accad's choice to not write extensively about her physical pain proves Scarry's claim that the descriptions of pain are few and, where they exist, approximate. This is why Lorde's elaborate descriptions of her phantom pain become especially powerful. Lorde's meditations bring the reader inside the body, emphasizing the fact of loss and the act of mourning and necessitating political responsibility. When Scarry interrogates the act of describing pain, she says "physical pain is not identical with (and often exists without) either agency or damage, but these things are referential; consequently we often call on them to convey the experience of the pain itself" (15). Scarry views the language of approximation as an inroad to describing pain, which is exactly what Lorde takes advantage of in her descriptions. She writes:

> On the morning of the third day, the pain returned home bringing all of its kinfolk. Not that any single one of them was overwhelming, but just that all in concert, or even in small repertory groups, they were excruciating. There were constant ones and intermittent ones. There were short sharp and long dull and various combinations of the same ones. The muscles in my back and right shoulder began to screech as if they'd been pulled apart and now were coming back to life slowly and against their will. My chest wall was beginning to ache and burn and stab by turns. My breast which was no longer there would hurt as if it were being squeezed in a vise. That was perhaps the worst pain of all, because it would come with a full complement of horror that I was to be forever reminded of my loss by suffering in a part of me which was no longer there. (38)

In Lorde's words, we find exactly what Scarry describes – approximations, temporal distinctions, and spatial distinctions. Lorde's words take advantage of this disintegration of language in that the approximations disorient rather than describe, confuse rather than clarify. After all, her body was not always home to the pain and its kinfolk. The different types of pain certainly do not conjure up the close-knit image alluded to with the term "kinfolk." Muscles also do not, as personified here, screech. This description of pain indicates the very inability to describe it and the excruciating prerequisite for such a loss of language. When juxtaposed with the laughing woman on the cover, this description of pain also highlights the multifaceted nature of dealing with cancer. In this moment, Lorde's text crystallizes the vacillation between feeling disempowered and feeling triumphant. She also, like Accad, amplifies Sontag's idea, demonstrating that the image can work alongside the narrative, rather than simply be undercut by it.

In Accad's narrative, the descriptions of physical pain are not present at all; she opts for simple declarations that pain has occurred: It hurts. It stings. Or, it burns. This omission of detail highlights the inability to articulate pain. Accad's silence coupled with the cover and her very detailed delineations of her treatment operate to emphasize the existence of her pain. It seems to surround the text, without being called upon explicitly. In so doing, Accad creates a discourse of pain not unlike that of Lorde's. Her minimal mention of it operates in the same way as Lorde's explicit mention of it in that both mark a disintegration of language. As I mentioned before, these gaps of eloquence in Accad have a critical utility. Given the verbosity of her text on other issues, particularly those that are the result of pain, like strained sexuality, strained patient-doctor relationships, and difficulty cultivating inner peace, this rhetorical reticence vis-à-vis physical pain underscores the existence of that pain and amplifies the existence of her psychological suffering (to which Accad does give voice).

Though Accad is silent about much of her physical pain and, to her friends, much of her psychological adjustment, she does not participate in the silencing of her own voice. What Accad experiences, at the hands of family, strangers, medical personnel and other healers, bears striking similarity to that of the tortured subject in Scarry's text. For Scarry, the tortured subject loses language just as the torturer doubles his language, hereby creating a silence for the tortured subject (36). She also argues that language can be taken away to immobilize the victim and undermine the possibility of representation. For Accad this occurs on several occasions. Within her doctors' offices, her doctors, specifically Dr. JE, deny her information or hide behind medical jargon, which usually results in her receiving poor care. Accad's sister, Adelaïde, calls cancer "Satanic" and admonishes Accad to repent; Adelaïde's commentary usurps Accad's understanding of her illness, so that she is at a loss for how to describe her life except in religious terms in the journal entries that follow. In both cases, Accad has not only undergone physical pain, but a theft at the level of language that removes her linguistic agency and places it in the hands of another. In her journal entries, Accad fights against these blanket narratives, by questioning their validity in relation to her experience. She writes against Dr. JE and Adelaïde's narratives to recuperate her own voice. Her desire to write against them echoes Lorde's text. Lorde contends that these types of silencing, these usurpations of one's own voice, are what forced her to write her text in the first place. She points out that silences enable fear and reduce the possibility of political action.

This disintegration and usurpation of language, in Scarry's view, serves to reify the power of the regime responsible for the torture. In Accad's and Lorde's narratives, to accept language as disintegrated and usurped would perform the same function as torture: reasserting the power of the medical establishment. However, Accad and Lorde stage a protest with their narratives, working against the dominant narratives of the health care industry. Their act of writing thwarts the ability of the regime to, as Scarry says, "translat[e] all the objectified elements of pain into the insignia of power, [and convert] the enlarged map of human suffering into an emblem of regime's strength" (56). For both of them, their pain transforms into the insignia of power, but it is their power. Their narratives reclaim agency and language as their own. To be specific, Accad draws on the discourse of the Holocaust ("never forget") and the necessity of survivors' stories in post-war Lebanon. The latter is the subject of one of her books, *Sexuality and War: Literary Masks of the Middle East*, and is, to be sure, a subject with which she is admittedly more familiar; nonetheless, she draws on both the Holocaust and the space of Lebanon to create parallels between women transnationally and cross-culturally. This link becomes especially important given the way in which she arrays research and cancer narratives from across the United States, Europe, and the Middle East. Lorde's text mobilizes the discourse of black queer feminist politics, emphasizing the multiplicity within identity categories. She demands that the government recognize the threat of environmental forces acting on the body rather than focus solely on the body as a site of cancer.

Both *The Wounded Breast* and *The Cancer Journals* continue Evelyne Accad and Audre Lorde's work as advocates of women of color. Their meditations on the experience of cancer and, in particular, the experiences of pain reimagine the narratives of illness. In their texts, the patient is not immobilized either physically or verbally; she is capable of political action and she resists the totalizing usurpation of her voice by a regime that neglects her under the guise of acting on her behalf. Accad and Lorde's critiques of the health care industry work toward a new understanding of illness itself, one that resists pandering to fear and demands agency for patients.

In their discursive acts of resistance, both Accad and Lorde challenge the notion of fragmentation most often touted by post-humanism. To amplify, post-humanism argues against the notion of the cogitating human as intrinsically different or, for lack of a better term, special. The field refuses to take humanity's uniqueness for granted, preferring instead to complicate our understanding of humanism by interjecting that humans share characteristics with animals and machines. In the case of Donna Haraway's landmark text, "A Cyborg Manifesto: Science, Technology, and the Socialist-Feminism in the Late Twentieth Century," the cyborg becomes a central figure for rethinking essentialism within multiple ontological categories and allowing those categories to do the political work of combating social and political discourse. Interestingly enough, Haraway's delineations of ontological categories does not include disability in any form.[5] It is precisely at this juncture that Accad and Lorde's texts trouble her work. Their texts raise the issue of the place of illness within this model of thinking. By positioning physical and psychological pain at the center of their political critique, Accad and Lorde disrupt the notion that you have to transgress boundaries in order to "explore [them] as one part of needed political work" (Haraway 154). They remain very much connected to their bodies as they participate in political work.

Specifically, Accad uses her body as the impetus for her political work. Her prose is guided by her intuition in many places and she explores multiple avenues of political activism and searches for some form of psychological balance. When discussing Bernie Siegel's work and her desire to cultivate inner peace, she mentions the environmental factors that she knows are involved in the proliferation of cancer (72). Her early journals link the Holocaust and cancer victims in terms of the scale of death (25); her later journals corroborate similar sentiments: namely, that cancer is akin to war (470-71). What is implicit in her link is that there is a responsible party. Though Accad does not specify, her suggestion aggregates her visceral response to her own mortality and her understanding of cancer as an epidemic to posit a critique of wide spread capitalism and a lackadaisical medical system.

Lorde's discussion of her choice to not wear a prosthetic directly challenges the notion of the cyborg in that Lorde refuses a prosthetic that would mask her experience of cancer. For her, the hybrid human/machine is not the answer, because the machine, in this case, the prosthesis, would erase the experience of the human. This is more than a humanist cry for the uniqueness of humanity; Lorde rejects the prosthesis because she is dissatisfied with the narrative it creates about the cohesion of humanity. From her purview, the prosthesis is another attempt at a totalizing narrative. The cyborg's merger between humans and machines ignores the extent to which the machine is forced onto her body in significant ways. In the case of the prosthesis, the machine is a mechanism of ostracization. After all, the original prosthesis is flesh-colored, but not the color of her flesh. In fact, the only skin tone it matches is that of white person's, specifically one whose flesh has pinkish undertones. Needless to say, this also leaves out other women of color and white women whose flesh has olive or golden undertones. The prosthetic also becomes a mechanism to create guilt and shame. The nurse's statement that her lack of prosthesis is bad for morale indicates that Lorde's acceptance of her own body disrupts the narrative of supposed normalcy created by prosthetics. In addition, the nurse's comments blame Lorde for not being a specific type of cancer survivor. Here, the machine emphasizes the very boundaries Haraway's cyborg is supposed to critique.

One critic, Diane Price Herndl, argues that Lorde's complaint about prosthetics has been changed by the advent of post-humanist thought. Herndl engages in a theoretical self-analysis to justify her own choice to wear a prosthetic and understand her choice in relation to her feminism. After chastising herself for making an anti-feminist decision vis-à-vis reconstruction, she notes, "I rethought what I meant by feminist theory and realized that feminist relations to the body are different now than they were twenty years ago for Lorde and that feminist relations to breast cancer are different" (149). This difference, she states, is due to post-humanism. Because the cyborg allows an understanding of oneself as already alien, the post-humanist feminist can embrace the prosthetic. Certainly, Herndl correctly identifies the differences between Lorde's historical moment and her own (circa 1999); however, millennial feminists still have to contend with narratives that privilege two breasts, more specifically two white perky B or C cup breasts between 18 and 25 and engaged in heterosexual coupling. This ideal, which still does not include women similar to Audre Lorde – black, with large breasts, well above the age of 25 and lesbian –, needs to be interrogated. Herndl's commentary obfuscates the ways in which a desire for the ideal and an adherence to it dictates the possibility of political critique. While I do not find Herndl's decision less than feminist, her rationale appears to minimize the way that reconstructive surgery reaffirms the status quo and silences some of the political critique available. Though Herndl's choice, in her mind, becomes a way to embrace the post-human, her joint kinship with machines, and her cyborg identity, it does not explore the vacuum of political critique created by her "partiality for a normal appearance" (151).

Herndl argues cogently that a masectomy scar and a reconstructed breast would be the same for her in that both remind her of her missing breast. She confesses, "prosthesis is technology, and it never lets me forget" (152). She understands that she will forever feel like Haraway's cyborg: not completely human, nor completely machine, but, certainly, alien and ready to voice a political critique. Here, Haraway's cyborg, in the form of Herndl, does perform necessary political work. Nevertheless, Herndl neglects a salient point in Lorde's critique of the prosthesis (and, by extension, reconstructive surgery): that her lack of prosthesis is not simply about how she conceives of her body, but how others understand her. Lorde understands prostheses as a barrier to forming support networks (16) and asks where are the black, lesbian, feminist role models for her (28-29). These remarks demonstrate that Lorde's choice was, in addition to being about her understanding of her own body, a matter of making herself recognizable to others. Lorde privileges her body's power to speak for itself, as a focal point for generating political power and creating viable communities. Inasmuch as a woman with reconstructed breasts can speak, as Herndl bravely chooses to do, she still has a visible disconnect between her body and her voice. This disembodiment subtracts from the possibility of critique and reinscribes the body into so-called normalcy.

What's more, the disconnect between embodied experience and disembodied voice ratifies silence. According to Elaine Scarry, hearing about someone's pain creates doubt, unlike the certainty of actually having pain (6-7). A reconstructed breast or a prosthesis positions the wearer to always create some modicum of doubt vis-à-vis her experience. Here, with the experience of cancer, the body is essential to expressing the certainty of that pain and the necessity of political mobilization. As with Evelyne Accad's book cover and the oft-cited Matuschka photo in the *New York Times Magazine*, the viewer cannot look away. For Accad and Lorde, there is no room for doubting their pain. Even when their language disintegrates, both women urge a meditation on their corporeal experience as an inroad to changing the medical system. They do ratify the ways in which their recovery hinges upon their relationship to machines and surgical procedures, but they refuse to allow technology to silence their embodied experience.

---

[1] Evelyne Accad's critical books *Sexuality and War: Literary Masks of the Middle East* (1990) and *Veil of Shame: The Role of Women in the Contemporary Fiction of North Africa and the Arab World* (1978) explore the differences between women's and men's narratives of war. The former posits that women's narratives demand an overhaul of contemporary attitudes vis-à-vis women's sexuality. The latter examines men's and women's narratives side by side, arguing that men's narratives are dismissive of an alternative to war, whereas women's narratives seek peace-keeping alternatives. Both have been critiqued and lauded for their idealism, breadth of scope and her illumination of Arab women's narratives regarding war. See Miriam Cooke, rev. of *Sexuality and War: Literary Masks of the Middle East*, by Evelyne Accad, and *Accommodating Protest: Working Women, the New Veiling and Change in Cairo*, by Arlene Elowe Macleod, *Middle Eastern Studies* 28.4 (1992): 812-14; Marilyn Booth, "Crossing the Demarcation Line," rev. of *Sexuality and War: Literary Masks of the Middle East*, by Evelyne Accad, *The Women's Review of Books* 8.8 (1991): 18; Margaret Fete, rev. of

Veil of Shame: The Role of Women in the Contemporary Fiction of North Africa and the Arab World, by Evelyne Accad, *The French Review* 53.2 (1979): 332-33; Issac Yetiv, rev. of *Veil of Shame: The Role of Women in the Contemporary Fiction of North Africa and the Arab World*, by Evelyne Accad, *Research in African Literatures* 10.3 (1979): 394-96. Audre Lorde's texts *A Burst of Light*, *Sister Outsider*, *Zami: A New Spelling of My Name*, and others are indicative of her long time commitment to complicating the essentialized version of woman, emphasizing her identity as multiple – black, lesbian, and feminist – and pointing to the virulence of totalizing narratives and institutionalized systems of oppression. See Alexis De Veaux, *Warrior Poet: A Biography of Audre Lorde* (New York: Norton, 2004).

[2] It is important to note that this text has had two covers: The original edition features Audre Lorde in the position I've described. The special edition features Audre Lorde smiling, with a scenic background, and the title is above her head.

[3] There is a great deal of conversation about the usefulness of pity within Disability Studies. Many scholars repudiate pity as a reaction that is infantilizing and not useful for changing social and political realities. Some view pity as a useful and necessary stepping stone to begin discussions on disability and disability rights. My main concern with Accad's book cover is that it seems to shun pity and validate the embodied experience of her missing breast. Precisely what I discuss in relation to Sontag's argument is that pity positions the object thereof as outside oneself and has the ability to create a space to assist and hear the subject or create a space to ignore the subject, a space that exists with a façade of interest or feigned support. The woman on the cover inhabits her own body, beckoning engagement, not dismissal.

[4] Sontag notes, "In the first of the six essays in *On Photography* (1977), I argued that while an event known through photographs certainly becomes more real than it would have been had one never seen the photographs, after repeated exposure it also becomes less real. As much as they create sympathy, I wrote, photographs shrivel sympathy. Is this true? I thought it was when I wrote it. I'm not so sure now. What is the evidence that photographs have a diminishing impact, that our culture of spectatorship neutralizes the moral force of photographs of atrocities?" (105). Sontag's questioning of her statement points to the idea that a photograph can linger – in the imagination and on the page – long after the photograph has been taken and viewed. Given the context, the photograph can also be reimagined and reinterpreted to multiple ends.

[5] It need be understood that disability is a vast field and I do not intent to conflate disability and illness here. Instead, I mention disability as a category that Haraway does not account for in her "informatics of domination."

Works Cited

Accad, Evelyne. *The Wounded Breast: Intimate Journeys through Cancer.* North Melbourne: Spinifex, 2001.

Alexander, Elizabeth. "'Coming out Blackened and Whole': Fragmentation and Reintegration in Audre Lorde's *Zami* and *The Cancer Journals.*" *American Literary History* 6.4 (1994): 695-715.

Bernie Siegel, MD. Ed. Bernie Siegel. 2008. 27 Oct. 2008 http:// www.berniesiegelmd.com

Haraway, Donna. *Simians, Cyborgs, and Women: The Reinvention of Nature.* New York: Routledge, 1991.

Herndl, Diane Price. "Reconstructing the Posthuman Feminist Body Twenty Years after Audre Lorde's *Cancer Journals.*" *Disability Studies: Enabling the Humanities.* Ed. Sharon L. Snyder, Brenda Jo Brueggemann, and Rosemarie Garland-Thomson. New York: Modern Language Association of America, 2002. 144-55.

Lorde, Audre. *The Cancer Journals.* San Francisco: Aunt Lute Books, 1980.

Morris, David B. "Un-forgetting Asclepius: An Erotics of Illness." *New Literary History* 38.3 (2007): 419-41.

Scarry, Elaine. *The Body in Pain: The Making and Unmaking of the World.* New York: Oxford UP, 1985.

Sontag, Susan. *Regarding the Pain of Others.* New York: Farrar, Straus and Giroux, 2003.

Robert McRuer

Submissive and Non-Compliant: The Paradox of Gary Fisher[1]

> The received wisdom, in straight culture, is that all of its different norms line up, that one is synonymous with the others. [...] If you deviate at any point from this program, you do so at your own cost. And one of the things straight culture hates most is any sign that the different parts of the package might be recombined in an infinite number of ways. But experience shows that this is just what tends to happen. If heterosexuality requires the entire sequence, then it is very fragile. No wonder it needs so much terror to induce compliance.
>
> (Michael Warner,
> *The Trouble with Normal: Sex, Politics, and the Ethics of Queer Life* 37-38)

> Even in his resistance, Fisher produced nothing like the independent, manly blackness that we see displayed in figures like [Frederick] Douglass. The gesture that Fisher illustrates – the black man with three, possibly four, fingers up his ass, the black man caught in an act of self-pleasuring (or self-degradation depending on one's point of view), the black man taking direction from the obviously self-deluded white – is hardly designed to rearticulate our most precious models of black subjectivity.
>
> (Robert F. Reid-Pharr,
> "The Shock of Gary Fisher" 141)

In 1996, Eve Kosofsky Sedgwick edited and published the journals and short fiction of her former student Gary Fisher. *Gary in Your Pocket: Stories and Notebooks of Gary Fisher* appeared three years following Fisher's death from HIV/AIDS. It is a return of sorts; in the words of Don Belton, who wrote the introduction to *Gary in Your Pocket*, the collection "is a resurrection of the power and seduction of Gary's conversation. It is a good vessel of Gary's voice" (xi). According to Belton, Fisher himself described that voice as the voice of a "black, queer sociopath" (qtd. in Belton ix). This self-description, presumably, in part alludes to the sexual fantasies and activities detailed throughout Fisher's writing. In the journal excerpts published in *Gary in Your Pocket*, most of the multiple sexual activities described, especially in the last few years of Fisher's life, are wrapped up in sadomasochistic fantasies; they are also often anonymous (with Fisher going nameless, using an assumed name, or taking on a label or identity such as "slave") and consummated in public or semi-public spaces. Fisher particularly returns quite often to Buena Vista Park near his apartment in San Francisco, but he also seeks encounters on the phone and – at least in a few of his final fantasies – in a reconstructed "kinky hospital" (251). Fisher's exploration of sexual domination and submission and a world of masters and slaves, moreover, often explicitly includes, in the excerpts published in *Gary in Your Pocket*, fantasies of racial degradation.

The rehabilitation of Gary Fisher has perhaps already begun, if I – through my epigraphs – approach him through others, through "experts" already skilled at analyzing such figures. Michael Warner and Robert F. Reid-Pharr are, of course, queer public intellectuals; in good faith, it is important to underscore that they consistently attempt to write non-compliance with heteronormativity, and affirmation of other ways of being, into existence. One paradox facing (and shaping) the queer public intellectual, however, is that she or he so often speaks or writes about challenges to authoritative systems like heteronormativity from authorized, and heteronormative, spaces (often, but by no means always, the small space for authoritative queer speech that has been forged, or granted, within the academy). Queer in the broadest sense, Warner and Reid-Pharr ensure, or assist me in ensuring, that "the shock of Gary Fisher" can still be registered. As authorities, however, they/we nonetheless inescapably mediate and (partially) rehabilitate him.

Approaching Fisher through "experts" contains him in ways that restore him to a rationality and intelligibility that he, paradoxically, constantly questioned or probed. Conversely, however, for me to approach Fisher unmediated – perhaps beginning with his raw sentiments that "sperm is addictive for niggers, as addictive as crack for niggers who can't see beyond the white goo" and that he is "PROUD TO BE A NIGGER" (239) – would also imply that he is (this time directly) knowable or containable in some way (and this particular passage, and my re-presentation of it, is disturbing because, on some level, we – when the "n word" is used – think "we know what that means").[2] To put forward such an implication of knowability would be, to adapt Reid-Pharr, "obviously self-deluded" on my part.

To return (Fisher) to a conventional structure seems both safe and unsatisfying. Fisher's capacity as a writer to put a reader or critic in such an impossible position attests to his literary and philosophical mastery, although to attest to his mastery is not exactly to honor his own stated (and apparently deepest) desires. Despite these conundrums, and however unsatisfying it may be, the structure of this essay is as follows: beginning at the end (of Fisher's life and of the journal selections Sedgwick has included in *Gary in Your Pocket*), I first consider crip critiques legible in regards to rehabilitation proper in Fisher's writing (that is, in regards to the therapeutic treatment he undergoes at various stages in the progression of HIV disease). Second, building on Reid-Pharr, I briefly weave these critiques into Fisher's sadomasochistic will to degradation, paying particular attention to what that will to degradation suggests about identity trouble more generally. Third, I turn to Marlon Riggs's film *Tongues Untied*, considering how Fisher unsettles the revolutionary (or perhaps rehabilitative) agenda of that film. I conclude with some – generative, as I hope – reflections on form and obsessive-compulsive disorder (OCD), not by any means to fix Fisher with an additional diagnosis but to affirm or validate his reflections on the limits of identity and identification. The traces of OCD discernable in what is potentially one of the most open-ended, uncontainable forms (the personal journal) illustrate well Fisher's work at and on the points where identity disintegrates. "I'm really going to have to burn this," Fisher writes at one point (143). Resisting the apparent compulsion to incinerate his words, Fisher still manages, paradoxically, to generate a text that is almost too hot to touch.[3]

Fisher is, arguably, not the best candidate for exemplifying disability critiques of rehabilitation, at least according to the dominant terms of a late twentieth-century disability identity politics: he was not out and proud; he was – instead – extremely closeted about his HIV status until very close to the end. "Over many years," Sedgwick explains in her Afterword to *Gary in Your Pocket*, Fisher "shared the knowledge with very few of even his close friends, until less than a year before his death when an acute health breakdown necessitated a long, frightening hospitalization" (275). Despite living in San Francisco and studying at Berkeley for most of his HIV-positive years, Fisher was not apparently incorporated into HIV/AIDS or disability community, even though it would be difficult to find locations in the United States with more vibrant or resistant communities organized around both identities, especially – in regards to HIV/AIDS – in the late 1980s and early 1990s.[4] At times, in fact, disability identification seems to consist, for Fisher, almost solely in what one could call his crip identification with Sedgwick: "it wasn't until after I was diagnosed with breast cancer in 1991 that we began to get real. [...] I remember describing to Gary what I'd experienced as the overwhelming trauma of half a year of chemotherapy-induced baldness," she writes (Afterword 279, 281); he writes (to her) in turn, "I had a small battle with KS [Kaposi's sarcoma] recently. The kimo [sic] made me ill even at such low dosages. I can't imagine. [...] I guess I need to talk to you" (qtd. in Afterword 279).

Fisher's connection to Sedgwick is nonetheless in some ways sufficient. If it takes at least two people to make a crip, there are certainly ways in which *Gary in Your Pocket* suggests that Fisher and Sedgwick school each other in the art of crip non-compliance:

> Eve reminded me of something I'd told a doctor whose question seemed too specific for any patient. [...] I told him: "Doctor, I'm sorry, I'm not all here. Maybe it's a defense mechanism, I don't know, but part of me has gone away." [...] Eve experienced the same defensive removal. (262)

Sedgwick writes elsewhere about her connection to communities of gay men living with HIV/AIDS – communities that had, over the course of the 1980s and 1990s, learned to question rigorously medical and scientific authority (*Tendencies* 12-15). The passages in *Gary in Your Pocket* that weave together her experiences and Fisher's provide intimate, touching illustrations of that connection: "I love it when she says 'lots of love to you' into my machine. I should answer immediately"; "I'll need Eve's help buying hats" (265, 266).

Of course, I'm approaching here a text that was edited by Sedgwick; given that *Gary in Your Pocket* was compiled after Fisher's death, Sedgwick could be read as more involved in constructing Fisher, herself as a figure in Fisher's story, and the relationship between the two, than Fisher himself. Clearly, however, Fisher and Sedgwick were more than aware of the ways in which their relationship could be read in straightforward and hierarchized terms: teacher/student, editor/author, (white) patron/(black) writer; they discussed these issues before Fisher's death. Sedgwick writes,

Gary and I were both very conscious of a history of white patronage and patronization of African American writers, the tonalities of which neither of us had any wish to reproduce. Sexuality was a place where Gary was interested in dramatizing the historical violences and expropriations of racism; friendship, authorship, and publication, by contrast, were not. (Afterword 285-86)

By foregrounding the teacher/student, patron/author relationship, Sedgwick puts it under erasure, as does Fisher in many ways, even if (or as) his desire to please his former teacher is often apparent ("She's on my case too. It's time to get busy and I'm still putzing" [265]). I argue even further, however, that – at the limits of these overdetermined and hierarchized relationships – *Gary in Your Pocket* accesses alternative (crip) possibilities. Among those possibilities is the multi-faceted and multi-authored critique of rehabilitation and will to degradation that the text/Fisher/Sedgwick puts forward.

There are many examples of this critique in the final journal entries included in *Gary in Your Pocket*. An entry dated June 17, 1993, however, provides a particularly good example of Fisher and Sedgwick's collective crip critique, even though Sedgwick is not mentioned in it. A woman that appears to be a social worker (but who might be simply a philanthropist-cum-social worker) comes into Fisher's hospital room. Fisher does not detail in this entry exactly what her role in the hospital is, but she seems to have some involvement in creating pleasant surroundings for hospitalized individuals. She begins to talk with Fisher about what he describes as "the rather awful impressionist print on the wall [that] looks like bad Seurat." The woman – who apparently purchased the print herself on a trip to Europe – "thought it would be relaxing." Fisher insists, point-blank, "It's not." Fisher does not, however, give the woman *herself* this sober, dismissive assessment; it is what he writes in his journal, along with the assertion that the print "detracts from the incredible view of the city that has sustained me for 3 weeks now" (267).

The *actual* exchange between the two, very different from the sentiments Fisher records in his journal, is significant enough to quote at length:

The old woman went on to detail the obvious – a woman [in the print] is walking what looks like a goat, taking him to be tethered she thinks. "Many patients in this room," she says, "have found this very relaxing." I'm sure she meant the picture in toto and not just walking the goat. She moved along so quickly in her remarks that I wasn't sure I was supposed

to speak but I finally commented that I liked the hedge and the grass because they remind me of home. They do not. Indeed the way they obscure
the houses of the street beyond them has bothered me (I don't believe she
ever looked at me, not even during her mundane greeting – the whole of it
was so rote as to be completely unmemorable and worth writing about only as a trophy to the hollowness of so much effort, action, and concern,
care – many, if not all, things medical! *and* so many of the caretakers.
Hollow!) – she then said: "I thank you for sharing that with me," and then
she left. I said thank you with a stinging sincerity, I hope. Were those last
words of hers dismissal or did she intend to pile my observation on top of
the others who'd said, collectively at least, the picture relaxed them?
(267-68)

Like Ralph Ellison's Invisible Man, Fisher overcomes the subject of this entry
with yeses, undermines her with grins, and agrees her to death and destruction.
In what is traceable, by the end, as a collective – if always spectral – refusal by
"many patients" to give the woman the relaxation and sincerity that she needs
and that the therapeutic, rehabilitative relationship requires (a collective refusal
that, of course, appears to be acquiescence), Fisher quickly learns his part here,
even if it is not immediately clear what the script would have him saying or
doing. Once he learns his predictable part, Fisher dutifully plays it, but through
his lie registers a victory against "all things medical" and rehabilitative, and
against the many sincere caretakers who need him to be a compliant patient.

   The spirit presiding over this scene, however, is not so much Ralph Ellison as Audre Lorde. In a famous scene in Lorde's *The Cancer Journals*, a well-
meaning representative from the organization Reach for Recovery comes into
Lorde's hospital room following her mastectomy. She offers Lorde "a soft sleep-
bra and a wad of lambswool pressed into a pale pink breast shaped pad." "Her
message," Lorde notes, "was, you are just as good as you were before because
you can look exactly the same" (42). Later, it becomes clear that Reach for Recovery expects this identity as generic sameness from all the women accessing
their services; Lorde is told when she goes to their offices that if she does not
wear a prosthesis it is "bad for the morale" of patients and of the organization
(59). In contrast to Fisher, Lorde does not directly lie and refuses the padded bra
with the pale pink pad, but like Fisher, she does confide some sentiments not to
the social worker but to her journal: "I looked away, thinking, 'I wonder if there
are any black lesbian feminists in Reach for Recovery'" (42).

Whether or not Fisher himself is directly drafting what Henry Louis Gates Jr. might call (as he does in regards to the relationship, across time and space, between Alice Walker and Zora Neale Hurston) one of "the most loving revision[s] [...] we have seen in the tradition" (255), it seems to me that Sedgwick – through her inclusion of this particular episode, from "the thousands of pages of notebooks and journals that Gary kept" (Afterword 287) – is. Which is not to suggest that Fisher's echo of Lorde is unintentional: his knowledge as a teacher and student of African American literature certainly makes such a connection plausible.[5] But what is even more clear is that, like many women with breast cancer, Sedgwick turns to *The Cancer Journals* for sustenance. In the year of Fisher's death (1993), in fact, she described the book as "an immensely important account of dealing with breast cancer in the context of feminist, antiracist, and lesbian activism" (*Tendencies* 13). I feel as confident, in fact, that Sedgwick intentionally writes Fisher's anecdote into a tradition that incorporates Lorde as Sedgwick herself feels confident that Henry James intentionally writes about anal pleasures. Of course, Sedgwick's defiant affirmation of intentionality in regards to James and anality is in the queer interests of what she terms "an audience desired" ("Inside Henry James" 138). The crip non-compliance that Fisher and Sedgwick author here, especially through the invocation of others who disidentified with their rehabilitation, likewise calls forth an audience desired. That audience is not desired – as with Fisher's and Lorde's social workers – for its docility or its boosterism in regards to "morale" but rather for its playfulness, trickery, and creativity. Lorde identifies the collective "love of women" ("the sweet smell of their breath and laughter and voices calling my name") as the force that sustains her through *The Cancer Journals* (39). The love of Sedgwick and a host of imagined others whose bodies, minds, and laughter are not ultimately contained or stilled by rehabilitative initiatives – the love of crips, in other words – sustains Fisher through his own hospital journals.

Even the entries that can most be interpreted through the lens of compliance contain its opposite and conjure up another audience, sometimes – to shift the meanings of audience – another kind of audience with the health care practitioner in question. In an entry dated May 19, 1993, and specifically composed as a letter to Sedgwick, Fisher – after saying that he hates his doctor for "my crazy symptoms" – suggests alternatively that he has "accumulated so much love and respect (maybe a little lust too) for this man that I will take his next prescription unquestioned – same way I used to have sex" (257-58). If taking a prescription unquestioned marks compliance as we think we know it, the remainder of Fisher's sentence unsettles such a conclusion, to say the least. To a figure identified as "Master Park" (presumably the same Park he later imagines calling up for "kinky [...] games" when he is hospitalized [251]), Fisher had written a few years earlier, "I enjoy being your nigger, your property and worshipping not just you, but your whiteness. [...] I really wanted your cum and more of your piss" (230-31). The doctor whom Fisher loves and hates is hearing little more than a "yes" when his prescription is dispensed, but Sedgwick (in the entry addressed to her) and readers of *Gary in Your Pocket* inescapably hear something quite different, given that numerous entries like the one to Master Park have preceded this medical scene. What looks like compliance on an ordinary day is something else altogether. Taking Fisher at his word here ("same way I used to have sex") means recognizing that his "yes" to the doctor contains the desire for degradation and that the doctor's prescription, to be taken in some sort of religious and sexual ecstasy, contains cum and piss.

Sometimes, however, Fisher's resistance is more straightforward, through wry, perceptive readings of medical or bureaucratic (in)efficiency. Saying that he "refused, sometimes wholesale" to follow a doctor's orders, that "they couldn't stick or poke or scan me in any way without my permission," Fisher quickly learns how things work and can immediately identify when "someone had fucked up" (261). When he informs his nurse that the doctors have made an error interpreting his symptoms and prescribing a solution, "she looked at me like I'd farted" (262). The nurse insists not only that an error would be impossible, given that "errors in this profession [...] could be costly," but also that Fisher is having headaches even though he says he is not. "My god, what if I made a mistake?" she says. "We can't change anything without a doctor's consent." Fisher replies simply, "You're making a mistake now" (262). Clearly aware that the system is not working, Fisher refuses to participate and lets this scene play out, until the nurse finally discovers that indeed an error has been made and offers "the most profuse apologies" (262).

At least once in the selections included in *Gary in Your Pocket*, Fisher directly and literally escapes from the Alta Bates Summit Medical Center where he is being treated. Alta Bates may offer "comprehensive services designed to meet the health care needs of the diverse communities of the greater East Bay Area" (Alta Bates, "About Us"), but Fisher – invoking the original *Psycho* – still calls it the "Bates Inn" (259). In this scene, he is literally identified (tagged, in fact) as a patient, but he takes pleasure in disguising that identity and resisting the complicated machinery that encompasses and indeed engenders the "AIDS patient." "Snuck out of Alta Bates," he writes,

> If my sleeve rises too high (I used the 2nd button) the white and gray ID bracelet will be noticeable to this keenly observant jewish fellow sitting next to me. Snuck out of AB, took off the throw-away smock, the ones with the 40 snaps that seem to fit any other 40 [...]. Took off all that stuff at Brad Lewis's urgence. He told me I'd have to sneak out, because not sneaking out would cost me my Medicaid coverage (which I don't really have anyway, yet). My last bill, by the way, was $18,000. I have to laugh whenever I look at it, all the procedures, chemicals and equipment I don't remember or understand. Just a strange concoction of symbols on 8-10 pages, two rows, the second one boasting amounts, and $5,470 for cancer drugs (in 5 days) would have to be a boast. (251)

Undoubtedly, the "needs" of the diverse communities Fisher moved through still exceed Alta Bates's capacity for "comprehensive services." The costs for HIV medication, conversely, have escalated to a point where Fisher's boast could be easily outdone by some later resident of the Bates Inn.

The laughter at economic and medical systems clearly designed with the interests of capital, not human beings, in mind, however, is to me the crux of this passage and the feature that most locates Fisher in crip traditions of non-compliance and even desertion. "Cripping," as Carrie Sandahl puts it, exposes "the arbitrary delineation between normal and defective and the negative social ramifications of attempts to homogenize humanity [...] disarm[ing] what is painful with wicked humor" ("Queering" 37). Sandahl does not specifically identify the economic system in which crips are currently located as among or grounding the things that are painful, but capitalism, infamously, does homogenize humanity, creating "a world after its own image" (Marx and Engels 477). Sandahl clearly connects cripping to alternative worlds and performances, however, which – as she suggests elsewhere – allow "for a multitude of imaginary identifications across identities" ("Black Man" 602). Thus, it is significant that Fisher escapes to a performative space of creativity, blackness, queerness, disability, and hope: leaving Alta Bates, he laughs and heads to the Alvin Ailey American Dance Theater (a dance troupe that was still thriving four years after Ailey's own death from complications due to AIDS) (Fisher 251).[6]

Laughing at, jarring, or exiting from systems of exploitation or oppression
are such longstanding black traditions that I have to question, on some level, the
Reid-Pharr assertion with which I opened this essay: that is, the idea that the
figure Fisher writes into existence "is hardly designed to rearticulate our most
precious models of black subjectivity." A good portion of Zora Neale Hurston's
career, to choose just one twentieth-century example, was dedicated to collecting and preserving (cherishing, making precious) the ways in which black subjects disarmed what was painful with wicked humor. In this tradition, and especially from a disability perspective, Fisher rearticulated, in multiple senses and
with virtuosity, powerful and resistant models of black subjectivity. Reid-Pharr,
however, does not exactly have the disabled and non-compliant Fisher in mind
in his argument, but the (seemingly) submissive Fisher, the figure Fisher himself
described as "a fit, intelligent black slave with a keen desire to please" (qtd. in
Sedgwick, Afterword 281). Despite the fact that I – engaged in the impossible
and perhaps self-deluded work of honoring him – have only approached this enslaved figure obliquely, he appears over and over again in *Gary in Your Pocket*:
"I want to be the TOY. [...] That's what being a faggot's all about, right?"
(188); "I'm on my knees again, before God. Tall, white, wary of me, trying to
work him into a froth of masterliness" (208); "The simplicity of it astounds me
and yet I have no words for it, just an image, at once holy and profane, of the
nigger on his knees taking cock juices into his body" (238-39).

Reid-Pharr's argument about this submissive figure is that he unsettles
"the philosophical and aesthetic ambitions of what has come to be known as
Black American culture," which turns "precisely on the necessity of establishing
a live blackness, a corporeality that does something other than announce social
death" (136). The "nigger corporeality" Fisher materializes, according to Reid-
Pharr, repudiates life on these terms and deliriously embraces death (135). Reid-
Pharr argues that Fisher forces a recognition that "there is no black subjectivity
in the absence of the white master, no articulation in the absence of degradation,
no way of saying 'black' without hearing 'nigger' as its echo" (137). I find
Reid-Pharr's theses largely convincing, despite my qualifications above (that is,
my contingent location of Fisher in vibrant black traditions). Indeed, I find Reid-
Pharr's assertions – which in part could be said to locate a will to degradation
operative in and through rehabilitation – largely in accord with or foundational
for my own. Rehabilitation, as Henri-Jacques Stiker and others have demonstrated, demands generic sameness and depends upon the aberration (128). I

contend that such demands and dependencies inevitably also attend late twentieth-century identity-movement conceptions of identity. "Even as we express the most positive articulations of black and gay identity," Reid-Pharr writes, "we are nonetheless referencing the ugly historical and ideological realities out of which those identities have been formed" (137). Fisher's articulation of "nigger pride" or embrace of "what being a faggot's all about," in other words, are not original to him; they can be traced even (or especially) in the locations that seem to oppose them the most.

It is not Reid-Pharr's subject, but there is a sense in which disability could claim a certain pride-of-place in what he is arguing, given that there is (literally) no way of articulating the very word "disability" in the absence of "ability" – and indeed, in the absence of the mastery that, as most would have it, naturally attends able-bodiedness. And, of course, to carry these points further, there is likewise no way of saying "disabled" without hearing "cripple" (or freak, or retard) as its echo. That there is no way of speaking the rehabilitated self without hearing the degraded other, however, is not a univocal fact. It is, instead, a fact in multiple ways. Identity depends on degradation in Reid-Pharr's sense – that is, resistant identities always reference the ugly historical and ideological realities from whence they emerged – but identity depends on degradation in another, redoubled sense: to the extent that identity-movement identities are rehabilitated identities ("gay is good [not bad]," "black is beautiful [not ugly]," "disabled and proud [not pitiful]"), they are also in some ways normative identities that inevitably incorporate generic sameness *in and through their distinctiveness* and that require and produce degraded others. This is not to deny a certain indispensability to the identity politics of the past few decades (indispensability conveying both necessity and unshakeability, regardless of our desires or intentions). It is, however, to locate and value (and in some ways, mourn) a certain rigor in projects like Fisher's that push the limits of such a politics, that appear in fact to be the most opposed to identity politics proper.

It is a rigor not always legible in *Tongues Untied*, and not simply because the "revolution" invoked by the film's famous concluding, and nation-building, thesis – Black Men Loving Black Men Is *The* Revolutionary Act – could be seen as in tension with the *reformist* history called up by the film's use of historic civil rights footage.[7] On the contrary: the film is in some ways, and ironically, *most* rigorous with that association; as Roderick A. Ferguson argues in *Aberrations in Black*, "liberal ideology captivates revolutionary nationalism" (3). In other words, revolutionary nationalism in the 1960s and 1970s inherited from reform movements a liberal failure "to conceptualize the multiple specificities and differences that constituted their various subjects" and indeed (again, like liberal reformism) "normalized the suppression of subaltern gender, racial, and sexual identities" (126). Although it does not directly test the limits of their respective political projects, *Tongues Untied* nonetheless makes visible these associations between reform movements and revolutionary nationalism.

If Ferguson's theses make it possible to apprehend these linkages in *Tongues Untied*, they also make accessible the film's (il)logic, its less rigorous moments. And what the film cannot know or acknowledge is, indeed, that aberrations in black are produced as necessary correlates of the non-aberrant (rehabilitated) black and gay revolutionary nationalists the film celebrates. Or, at least, in this case, aberrations in black leather: the SM subcultures of San Francisco – undoubtedly captured by the camera during the very years Fisher and other black, Latino, and Asian men he writes about were active members of them – are filmically constructed as necessarily both degraded and degrading. Fisher cannot be a black gay man because of his will to degradation; according to the logic of the film, which in an autobiographical sequence has Riggs fleeing Castro and Market Street cultures, a normative black gay identity comes only from exiting the spaces where Fisher, or traces of Fisher, or crips like Fisher, might be found.[8]

As John Champagne writes, in the analysis of *Tongues Untied* that first broached the ways in which it demonizes SM subcultures, "This granting of a subjectivity necessarily depends [...] on the figure of the undisciplined gay and lesbian body, who continues to act as a foil for a normal that can make sense only in terms of what it is not" (84). A foil for the normal in so many ways, seeking out/desiring undisciplined bodies, Fisher took pleasure in what Jeffrey J. Cohen calls a "historically specific masochistic *assemblage*, an intersubjective sexuality that almost always involves a transposition of institutionalized dominance and submission into unexpected arenas of performance" (79). Ironically, *Tongues Untied* – at least through its concluding thesis about black men loving black men and *the* (singular) revolutionary act – can be read as forwarding both an intersubjective sexuality and *expected* arenas of performance. Or, we might say (according to a strict reading of this thesis), an intersubjective sexuality performed in expected (rehabilitated) arenas – this particular revolution, in other words, expects compliance. Reading Fisher alongside *Tongues Untied* makes clear that he cripped rehabilitative agendas even before he was disabled.

Conclusion: "It's a big big room and it's full of everybody's hope I'm sure"

This is not a diagnosis. Nor is it intended to provoke a rehabilitation. With such disclaimers (or perhaps tributes to Magritte) in the background, however, one could argue that, sprinkled throughout Fisher's writing, there are traces of OCD: lines signifying new beginnings, outlines marking the rigid form future entries will or should take, worries he cannot shake about who might be reading him, obsessive questions about tense or punctuation. To cite just a few of the dozens of possibilities: "Neatness seems to inspire me. I'm not sure why" (123); "That's not the way it was supposed to be. […] [T]here won't be any more of what happened today" (139): "It's time to set some guidelines for this journal and future ones. This may be a conglomeration of materials, but its point is to show my daily progression and/or regression" (142): "Boy, tense still scares me – the most basic tool of my trade and I can't be sure" (270). I do not find these examples interesting because they fix Fisher, but because they show Fisher himself working or testing the limits. In the space of the personal journal, where he could, conceivably, enjoy a sort of limitless freedom (at least from written form or order), Fisher hems himself in, worrying about and working over the tiniest things. And yet, simultaneously, there are conversely innumerable entries (often the ones most ecstatically describing sexual activities) where such concerns about form, order, syntax, and punctuation – not to mention the cultural grammar of rehabilitation – appear to be deliberately repudiated ("I AM PROUD TO BE A NIGGER," in particular, marking an entry that concludes with no period, no punctuation).

Reid-Pharr writes that he is "not attempting to rehabilitate Fisher for those wary of perverse black subjectivity. On the contrary, Fisher's genius turns on his ability to spoil all our expectations, to deform our most cherished models of human subjectivity" (141). Reid-Pharr's piece is not in conversation with disability studies, though he does reverse here, in a potentially generative way, the usually negative metaphorical use of "deform." I do wonder, however, from a position internal to disability studies and the disability rights movement, whether the rehabilitation of Fisher (or anyone) can be so easily disclaimed, whether – in fact – the OCD-like moments in his journal position even Fisher himself both claiming and disclaiming rehab. Even if, as Reid-Pharr and numerous other queer theorists would have it, we must be able to grapple with the spaces where identity unravels, with what we might call the myriad crip forms that identity trouble takes, we still inhabit a world sedimented with rehabilitative logics speaking us.

Of course (and this is itself an OCD insight), the obsessive discipline that marks rehabilitation and the grandiose repudiation of that discipline could be seen as of a piece. And indeed, it's not difficult to see Fisher's worry over minutiae as simply the inverse of his at times Whitmanian (or perhaps Whitmanic) efforts to think and write differently, expansively: "I want to write large. Don't I want to write large?" (271). Fisher's big big room full of everybody's hope is one such expansive effort; it is the impossible space he imagined five months before he died, in an entry (the last one included in *Gary in Your Pocket*) dated September 19, 1993. "40 million people will have it by the end of the decade," Fisher writes, "I'm in good company. I'm in plenty of company. I'm less afraid. It's a big big room and it's full of everybody's hope I'm sure" (272). Fisher was actually quite close in his projections: in the year 2000, an estimated 36 million people globally were living with HIV/AIDS, 3 million died, and 5.3 million were newly infected. Almost 22 million people had already died by 2000, the vast majority of them non-white and without access to protease inhibitors or other therapies.

What I have written about *Gary in Your Pocket* does nothing to change these other stories. Put differently, what I have written does nothing to change these staggering numbers that are now part of history. I can, however, imaginatively put myself in Fisher's place: 50 million people will have it by the end of the decade. That future story can be changed, and the questions about identity, community, rehabilitation, and political economy that *The Transformation* and *Gary in Your Pocket* raise – questions about who is encompassed when "marginalized groups [...] render themselves visible" and who is not, and why (Champagne 70); questions about how to materialize what David Harvey calls "spaces of hope" and who is currently shut out of spaces that matter, and why—invite that change.

Rehabilitated identities, however necessary or inescapable, are not sufficient for making Fisher's big big room, which invokes that post-1996 story, accessible. But *Gary in Your Pocket* does keep in play some of the most important and ongoing challenges of crip theory, or more simply of progressive queer and disability movements at the turn-of-the-century: the challenge of always imagining subjects beyond LGBT or disability visibility, tolerance, and inclusion; the challenge of shaping movements that, regardless of how degraded they are, can value the traces of agency, resistance, and hope that are as legible where identity disintegrates as where it comes together.

---

[1] This essay is a shorter version of the chapter "Noncompliance: *The Transformation*, Gary Fisher, and the Limits of Rehabilitation," from my 2006 monograph *Crip Theory: Cultural Signs of Queerness and Disability* (103-46). Used with permission from the publisher, NYU Press.

[2] My invocation of "we know what that means" is of course not to suggest that "nigger" does not have multiple valences – on the most obvious level, the term historically has incredibly different valences for white and black speakers, and in majority white or majority black speaking contexts (for a discussion of the term's multiple valences, see Kennedy). Fisher's deployment of the term is highly ambivalent – regardless of who "we" are, we think "we know what that means" and Fisher is disturbing because he exceeds what we think we know.

[3] It is perhaps premature, less than a decade after its publication, to make pronouncements on the amount of critical attention to Fisher. Nonetheless, despite the fact that the publication context for *Gary in Your Pocket* – connected so directly to Sedgwick's work as both teacher and queer theorist, located in the prestigious Series Q from Duke University Press, introduced by Belton, blurbed by Marilyn Hacker and Randall Kenan – could hardly be more conducive for critical attention, Reid-Pharr's essay remains the only significant consideration of it. On this theme, Reid-Pharr writes, "I have been struck by how difficult the text seems to have been for those people – white, black, and otherwise – who have encountered it. Indeed responses have ranged from righteous indignation toward the text and its editor […] to a rather maddening inarticulateness" (149).

[4] On the inception of disability movements in Berkeley, see Shapiro 41-73. For an oral history of the AIDS Epidemic in San Francisco, see Shepard.

[5] According to Sedgwick, Fisher began graduate work at Berkeley in 1984: "Continuing to live in San Francisco and commute across the bay, he did well in graduate school, was admitted to the Ph.D. program after three semesters, became a gifted teacher of composition and of American and African-American literature, and developed strong friendships with a few other graduate students" (Afterword 274). A few of the journal entries included in *Gary in Your Pocket* represent Fisher working through complex issues of race, desire, and power in American literature, most notably an entry dated January 31, 1987, attempting to answer the question "where's a black reader's desire?" in Herman Melville's "Benito Cereno" (201). Fisher writes in this entry of the pleasure in what he calls "the S and M game" in "Benito Cereno" and links that game to the complicated (and deadly serious) play of domination and submission in other texts, including William Faulkner's *Light in August* and Richard Wright's *Native Son* (201-03).

[6] I'm calling the Alvin Ailey American Dance Theater a space of disability because of how thoroughly it has remained associated with Ailey's legacy and indeed with HIV/AIDS. Fisher himself associates it with both as he writes about leaving the Alta Bates Summit Medical Center to

attend a performance. Fisher's timeline in this journal entry, incidentally, is slightly off – he writes (in 1993) that Ailey had died eight years earlier; it had only been four. Alvin Ailey died in 1989 at the age of 58. The Alvin Ailey American Dance Theater continues to thrive today.

[7] I find *Tongues Untied* to be one of the richest and most teachable texts of the LGBT 1990s, and have used it in the classroom innumerable times since its release. However, the first time I taught *Tongues Untied* next to Fisher (or – true confessions – next to Fisher mediated through Reid-Pharr's essay on him), my students were tellingly tongue-tied. The first effect of the juxtaposition, in other words, was a difficult and extended silence in the classroom – which was then followed by one of the best class discussions I have ever experienced. My thanks to the members of my Queer Cultural Studies class from Fall 2002, in particular Nathan Weiner and Miriam Greenberg.

[8] I am drawing attention here to the ways in which men of color participate in SM subcultures partly because Fisher seems to me to have consistently noticed their participation; on this point, then, I read *Gary in Your Pocket* slightly differently from Reid-Pharr who suggests that men of color are "hailed" only "infrequently" in Fisher's text (143). It is not only the journal entries, moreover, but the stories included in the first half of *Gary in Your Pocket*, that suggest that Fisher's San Francisco years were marked by careful observation of both white people and people of color and by constant theorizing about how little about race, gender, sexuality, and embodiment is apparent on the surface of quotidian relations and conversations.

Works Cited

Alta Bates Summit Medical Center. "About Us." *Alta Bates Summit Medical Center*. 6 Feb. 2005 <http://www.altabates.com/about/>.

Belton, Don. Introduction. *Gary in Your Pocket: Stories and Notebooks of Gary Fisher*. Ed. Eve Kosofsky Sedgwick. Durham: Duke UP, 1996. vii-xii.

Champagne, John. *The Ethics of Marginality: A New Approach to Gay Studies*. Minneapolis: U of Minnesota P, 1995.

Cohen, Jeffrey J. *Medieval Identity Machines*. Minneapolis: U of Minnesota P, 2003.

Ferguson, Roderick A. *Aberrations in Black: Toward a Queer of Color Critique*. Minneapolis: U of Minnesota P, 2004.

Fisher, Gary. *Gary in Your Pocket: Stories and Notebooks of Gary Fisher*. Ed. Eve Kosofsky Sedgwick. Durham: Duke UP, 1996.

Gates, Henry Louis, Jr. *The Signifying Monkey: A Theory of African-American Literary Criticism*. New York: Oxford UP, 1988.

Harvey, David. *Spaces of Hope*. Berkeley: U of California P, 2000.

Kennedy, Randall. *Nigger: The Strange Career of a Troublesome Word*. New York: Pantheon, 2002.

Lorde, Audre. *The Cancer Journals*. 2nd ed. San Francisco: Aunt Lute, 1980.

Marx, Karl, and Friedrich Engels. "Manifesto of the Communist Party." 1848. *The Marx-Engels Reader*. 2nd ed. Ed. Robert C. Tucker. New York: Norton, 1978. 469-500.

McRuer, Robert. *Crip Theory: Cultural Signs of Queerness and Disability*. New York: New York UP, 2006.

Reid-Pharr, Robert F. "The Shock of Gary Fisher." *Black Gay Man: Essays*. New York: New York UP, 2001. 135-49.

Sandahl, Carrie. "Black Man, Blind Man: Disability Identity Politics and Performance." *Theatre Journal* 56.4 (2004): 579-602.

---. "Queering the Crip or Cripping the Queer? Intersections of Queer and Crip Identities in Solo Autobiographical Performance." *GLQ: A Journal of Lesbian and Gay Studies* 9.1-2 (2003): 25-56.

Sedgwick, Eve Kosofsky. Afterword. *Gary in Your Pocket: Stories and Notebooks of Gary Fisher*. Ed. Eve Kosofsky Sedgwick. Durham: Duke UP, 1996. 273-91.

---. "Inside Henry James: Toward a Lexicon for *The Art of the Novel*." *Negotiating Lesbian and Gay Subjects*. Ed. Monica Dorenkamp and Richard Henke. New York: Routledge, 1995. 131-46.

---. *Tendencies*. Durham: Duke UP, 1993.

Shapiro, Joseph P. *No Pity: People with Disabilities Forging a New Civil Rights Movement*. New York: Times Books, 1993.

Shepard, Benjamin. *White Nights and Ascending Shadows: A History of the San Francisco AIDS Epidemic*. London: Cassell, 1997.

Stiker, Henri-Jacques. *A History of Disability*. 1997. Rev. ed. Trans. William Sayers. Ann Arbor: U of Michigan P, 1999.

Tongues Untied. Dir. Marlon Riggs. Frameline Distribution, 1989.

Warner, Michael. *The Trouble with Normal: Sex, Politics, and the Ethics of Queer Life*. New York: Free, 1999.

Ned Mitchell

Sexual, Ethnic, Disabled, and National Identities in the "Borderlands" of Latino/a America and African America

In this project, I will examine Piri Thomas's *Down These Mean Streets* (1997) and Susana Aiken and Carlos Aparicio's *The Transformation* (1996) and the ways in which the sexual, ethnic, disabled, and national identities presented are mutually constitutive in the "borderlands" of latino/a America. The Anzalduan "border subject" has enabled a conception of inhabiting the "borderlands" and reading it as a generative "third-space." Ironically, it can be argued through these texts that inhabiting the "impossible" space of the border may actually be more possible (or preferable) than attempting to inhabit the identities which are demanded by the forces of Christianity, "Americanization," normalization, and more generally, the constraints of global capitalism that call into existence such forces. If the impossible space of the border has been largely discussed in relation to U.S. Latino/a cultures, however, this paper opens onto a consideration of the borderlands of African America. I argue that black modernities have always been central to the construction of the border subject (although that centrality has at times been marked most prominently by repudiation, as the protagonist in *Down These Mean Streets* rejects his blackness and embraces a distinctively white Christianity).

The matrix of forces identified here are indeed always/already oppressive in their material manifestations and an escape from such machinations is not imagined as material or identifiable except within the logic (or illogic) of the third-space inhabited. As such, I will attempt to read against the grain the narrative of failure that is located in the subject of both of these texts (in *Down These Mean Streets*, implicitly, and *The Transformation*, explicitly; and in a particularly overdetermined narrative of HIV/AIDS, most problematically) and instead posit that the "failure" here is a failure of global capitalism to successfully colonize, to make intelligible, these border subjects. In this sense, their position in/on the border has enabled an immaterial liberation of self that functions because of/despite material oppression.

I should not go any further without addressing my own apprehension that, in dealing with the personal and the autobiographical, I am transforming these people into powerless subjects that will bend and sway to my own universalizing impulse. The pain, physical and emotional, expressed through these narratives should not be ignored. Ricardo/Sara and Piri Thomas are real people, and were often willful participants in what I (seemingly cynically) might call their "subsumption." I make every attempt to read their stories respectfully, both as they seem to me and, perhaps more importantly, as they might have been. So I am not a just spectator to their stories, or an author, but I find in their stories an experience of oppression unique to them and a way of oppressing familiar to many. There are many ways to read these texts and there may be value in confusion and possibility in ambiguity.

The Revolution of Sara to Ricardo – and Back

> The thing that makes [Ricardo] unusual is that he is enormously charismatic. He attracts people, he has power, he has presence, he has personality – as they say, he could sell tennis shoes to a paraplegic. That kind of personality. But there was something missing. And what was missing, is that he never knew what it was to be a man.

These are the concluding lines to the opening monologue about Ricardo spoken by Terry, the man who first encountered the drag queens living in the salt mines and began the work of "transforming" them with the help of his fundamentalist Christian congregation in Dallas, Texas. The film presents the story of Ricardo as a journey from living as a transgendered woman in the salt mines through moving to Texas, converting to Christianity, "transforming" into a man and marrying another woman in the congregation, and eventually the fatal effects of his HIV, which has developed into full-blown AIDS. That is the physical journey presented, but the film also represents a metaphorical journey between two seemingly opposing and excluding identities. Unpacking even this seemingly forthright statement from Terry takes some work: Ostensibly he is talking about his affection for the man he knows as Ricardo – except the man he knows is not a man at all, having lived much of his/her life until meeting Terry as a woman. Terry tells us, in fact, that he (Ricardo) "never knew what it was to be a man." So Terry must actually be talking about Sara, a woman whose identity he repeatedly and insistently rejects by calling her "he." This confusion over who or what Ricardo and Sara "really" are is not a simple linguistic complication. It is the central problem of the film and is constantly addressed, re-confused, and then subsequently ignored. Ricardo and Sara, as one individual, cannot function in the logic of the heteronormative system they are asked to inhabit. As Robert McRuer points out in his reading of the film, Sara continues to be present in the film even after she is physically dispensed with at the beginning. He shows how the impossibility of certain scenes might have been mediated by Sara's presence. That is to say (and I use his words in a broader sense), "*Sara* might have understood [...] but Ricardo cannot" (131, my italics).

I try to avoid replicating the excellent analysis of the film by McRuer in his book *Crip Theory*, but instead use that analysis as a starting point for a deeper reading of how Ricardo and Sara are constituted as "revolutionary" ("transformative") subjects of the late capitalist moment. The religious conversion mirrors the capitalist transformation, changing a "fallen" and "marginal" individual subject into a redeemed, productive, normatively sexual member of the church and member of the "society" that is manifest to the church congregation and the others around Ricardo.

Revolution's "Men"

In Ricardo Ortiz's "other" history of the Cuban Revolution, he at one point identifies the "imbedded homophobia" in the discursive practices surrounding the revolution. He rightly remarks that the repeated use of the pronoun "'Ours' [...] evokes the sense of community and solidarity among persons and groups of persons to which perhaps most of us strive; on the other, darker side, it inevitably effects that happy inclusion by some necessary exclusion" (36). Citing Brad Epps, Ortiz identifies this practice as a mode of sexual (dis)empowerment that is in itself homophobic:

> While the Cuban revolution seeks a surrender of the individual to the collective, a sacrifice of the ego to the (ego) ideal, it refuses what it sees as a surrender, in the flesh as in the mind, of one man to another. While the former "surrender" is understood in terms of empowerment (I surrender to the I to be stronger in and as the We), the latter is understood in terms of disempowerment, degradation and abjection (I surrender to another, stronger I). (36)

Ortiz, for various reasons, avoids fully addressing this idea outright and instead sets it off through a catalog of the ways in which "anti-revolutionary" politics were cast as a form of sexual deviance in the literature of the period. But a more immediate reading of this idea can be found in the practices as well as the discourses represented in the texts *Down These Mean Streets* and *The Transformation*.

Most pointedly, the prospect of religious "salvation" offered and accepted (at least temporarily) by both Ricardo/Sara and Piri casts "surrender to the we" as the ultimate "transformative" that will make their manhood complete, by transforming Sara into Ricardo and by freeing Piri from the emasculating circumstances of prison life. In *The Transformation*, Jim and Robby are charged with the task of literally teaching Sara (now Ricardo) "how to be a man." To Jim, this means showing him how to do "manly things" such as mow the lawn or fix things around the house or "anything physical." On the surface, and to Jim and ostensibly Ricardo, this process is self-evident and self-justifying: there are certain things that "men" do in this time and place, and Ricardo has never done them before so he must be taught. He assumes the place of the male child of Jim and Robby (who are childless) and presents a challenge: Jim must prove himself by helping Ricardo discover his own latent masculinity. But this is complicated by Epps' work, as Ricardo seems to be "surrendering" to Jim. Jim is "saved" by the fact that he has reluctantly accepted this task as a way of furthering his own surrender to the church – he says, "we were supposed to kinda take him under our wing and try to help disciple him." The failure of Ricardo to fully transform, then, is a failure of Jim's to revolutionize him, as we find out that Ricardo would ultimately prefer to have remained Sara. Recall that the gospel that is preached throughout the film is undermined by the very act of "teaching Ricardo how to be a man," which admits that Sara was not a man at all – the fact that she required this intervention (and that Sara continued to exist) firmly establishes her location in the third-space.[1]

Ricardo, then, seems to lack any agency whatsoever in his own transformation. And to a certain extent, he does – his success depends on surrender to the church, to God, to higher powers that can remake him. One key scene is when we first see Ricardo as he is post-transformation. He is in a prayer circle with several members of the church including his wife Betty and the man who first "took him into his home and discipled him," Jim. Ricardo, in English (up until now we have only heard Sara speaking Spanish), is thanking Jesus Christ

for "the people around" him, for his wife Betty, for Jesus' "help financially, everything." Then Jim begins a prayer on Ricardo's behalf, saying,

> Father, we just thank you for the *change* in Ricardo and in his life. Father,
> we thank you that you have brought him from such a, such a deep and
> dark hole, Lord, but that you have lifted him up out of that place. Father,
> you have set him up, Lord, You have stuck him in the devil's face and
> you have said, "*Look*, at what I can do [...]." We see the transformation
> taking place even now, Lord, and we thank you for that transformation in
> Ricardo's life and in his heart. (Vocal emphases in original)

Of course, praising what Ricardo has "become" is not enough – it is necessary to
denigrate what he "was," that is, Sara. This abjection, in the sense of "degradation" and "absolute and humiliating," occurs over and over in the film and in
Thomas' narrative. In a sense, then, these layers of degradation (Jim, before
God, Ricardo, before Jim and God, Gigi, before Ricardo) and abjection serve as
an able metaphor for the pyramid scheme politics of transformation that haunt
the film. Ricardo and the other transgendered people of the salt mines are ve-
hicles to satisfy the fundamentalist/evangelist logic of proselytization that ensures them a place in heaven. Both the Cuban revolution and the church offer a
reward in the form of a larger, stronger We, the difference being that the revolution's reward is corporeal while one can be sure Sara's (and Ricardo's) degradation by the church will continue as long as he lives.

In this abjection and degradation, however, lies part of Ricardo's agency.
He is torn between those who see the abjection identified above (and throughout) as necessary and those who see that abjection as abject in itself, in the sense
of self-abasing. When Gigi, one of Sara's friends from the salt mines, is shown
pictures of Ricardo, she immediately says, "What a killer you are, Sara. [...] She
looks so changed." There is no doubt in Gigi's mind about who Sara is, and she
insistently calls Ricardo "Sara" throughout the film. Terry, Jim, and the rest
must either ignore the ambiguity around Ricardo/Sara or confront it by abjecting
Sara, eliminating the possibility that she continues to exist (and she does, for
Gigi, Giovanna, and ultimately, Ricardo).

As McRuer points out, Gigi and another character, Giovanna, are presented as foils to Ricardo. Giovanna, who is not HIV positive, lived with Sara in
the salt mines but recently moved back into an apartment with her mother,
brother and sister. While her brother is absent from the film, her mother and sister seem to have completely adapted to Giovanna's identity and even embrace it,

as in the scene where Giovanna and her sister attend a costume party dressed as Hollywood starlets from the 1950s. Gigi and Giovanna, while they cannot bring themselves to endorse Sara's choice to transform, understand her very real need for access to care and treatment for her disease (Gina says, "Finding out he was HIV positive changed him. [...] The church was the only way out."). Reading between the lines, though, they hint at what McRuer identifies as the "dignity [that] attends Sara's living situation, according to a broad reading of Braverman's terms: on the level of gender, sexual desire, community, behavior" (123). He cites *The Trouble With Normal*, saying that this dignity "is inherent in the human. You can't, in a way, not have it" (Warner 36). In short, those who see Ricardo's choice to transform as abject understand his reasons for doing so, but lament the price he had to pay to get medical care. This understanding is not reflected by those who effected his transformation, as their "charity" comes with a very steep price: the surrender of the dignity inherent in the human.

On The Beaten Path

Down These Mean Streets is an autobiographical account of the first three decades of Piri Thomas' life, beginning with his childhood in Spanish Harlem in New York City through his later imprisonment for shooting a police officer and his eventual release. He is the son of Puerto Rican emigrants and like his father has a significantly darker complexion than the rest of his family. As such, he is constantly trying to negotiate and affirm his Puerto Rican identity despite the general perception of him outside the Puerto Rican community as an African American. He is also, at the same time, confusing and re-enforcing the boundaries of his masculinity as an "independent man" in the vein of the revolutionary subject. In his personal narrative, he has always and will always refuse to "surrender" to another man. Yet several events in the book as well as telling reflections in his personal narrative show that this refusal is in reality a denial of desires that are already present. I will demonstrate how ideas similar to those Ortiz finds imbedded in Cuban Revolutionary sexual politics play out in multiple places in Thomas' narrative.

Piri's first obvious encounter with queer sexualities is when he is a young teenager and, with several of his male friends, goes to visit "the faggots' apartment" (they are, as it turns out, male transvestites) and have sex with them in exchange for money and drugs. After all of the boys reluctantly (and wordlessly, as none of them wants to be the first to agree to the idea) decide to go to the apartment, Piri tries to convince himself not to "cop out" in spite of the fact that

> I don't wanna go! I don't wanna go! Shit, imagine getting your peter pulled like a motherfuckin' straw! I don't wanna go – but I gotta, or else I'm out, I don't belong in. And I wanna belong in! Put *cara palo* on, like it don't move you. (55)

Piri's desire to assert his masculinity through belonging to a stronger, more masculine group of peers outweighs his desire to avoid homosexual contact. Ordinarily, homosociality (apparently the relationships among Piri and his friends) is protected from homosexuality by homophobia. But in this instance the threat of losing that homosociality and the collective masculinist affirmation that goes along with it outweighs the individual threat to Piri's masculinity. "Cara palo," meaning literally "face stick," that is, face like a stick, also the violent connotation of "caerle a palos," to fall on someone with sticks. The violence of forcefully pushing down latent desires (or fears of those desires) is implied here, again recalling the assertive physical violence Piri uses to claim his masculinity throughout his childhood.[2] Later, after Concha has given Piri oral sex (throughout which Piri is saying to himself, "*I like broads, I like* muchachas, *I like girls*" [61]), he leaves the apartment "to wash [his] nose out from all that stink" (61) and reflects on the experience:

> I felt strong and drained. I hadn't liked the scene, but if a guy gotta live, he gotta do it from the bottom of his heart; he has to want it, to feel it. It's no easy shake to hold off the pressure with one hand while you hold up your sagging pants with the other. But the game is made up as you go along. (62)

This ambiguity is central to Piri's personal construction of masculinity. He desires validated masculinity so much ("he has to want it, to feel it") that any "trial" that risks his masculinity is safe, so long as afterwards he can claim "success" or victory in the face of it. "The game is made up as you go along," he says. He is somehow stronger for having allowed himself to surrender so completely. He will return to the idea expressed in his last statement again and again, constituting his masculinity as avoidance of those who are "anti-revolutionary," that is to say homosexuals, prisoners, women, and as a surrender to a larger and larger revolutionary "We" that can validate and transform him into a "new" or "real" man.

In a similar sense, Piri's encounter with the criminal justice system is an encounter with the logic imbedded in the politics Epps is critiquing, and in my opinion, another failure of that logic. Piri's masculinity is secure in prison by his constant assertion that it is located outside prison; that is to say, he must bear his prison experience "like a man" and survive "intact" in order to reclaim his proper place in the "free" world. Specifically, this means avoiding having sex with men, and more generally, it requires "admitting" his love for God, even if God doesn't "belong" to him, because

> *If God is right, so what if he's white?* I thought, *God, I wanna get out of this hole. Help me out. I promise if you help me climb out, I ain't gonna push the cover back on that cesspool. Let me out and I'll push my arm back down there and help some other guy get a break.* (323)

Similar to Ricardo's situation, Piri's situation pre-transformation is figured as a "hole," or "cesspool" that he can escape only by surrendering his agency and individuality to the conditional love of God, who may or may not help him, and asks in return that he pass on the message of conditional love. Ricardo must also repay his debt, by going on the road with Terry to speak about his transformative experience (which we do not see in the film), as well as go back to "the streets" and try to convince Gigi and Giovanna to "come off the streets" because they (the Christian ministry) have "a place for them." What McRuer calls an essential part of "rehabilitation" (122), I identify as also a part of "revolution" or "transformation" – the need not only to transform oneself but to "degrade" oneself in the work of transforming others. Piri, by "pushing his arm back down there" (implying resistance) and Ricardo by degrading Sara publicly, both abject parts of their self in order to effect a complete transformation.

In Piri's first meditation on sex in prison, he finds himself at war with himself to resist the temptation of "marrying" a "faggot" named Claude, who pursues him relentlessly, promising Piri all of the benefits of "marriage." Piri resists this precisely as a temptation rather than an affront:

> I looked past the green bars at Claude and saw a woman's pleading, tormented face. *He wants to buy a daddy-o,* I thought. *But I ain't gonna break. One time. That's all I have to do it. Just one time and it's gone time. I'll be screwing faggots as fast as I can get them. I'm not gonna get*

> *institutionalized. I don't want to lose my hatred of this damn place. Once*
> *you lose the hatred, then the can's got you* [...] *Outside is real; inside is a*
> *lie. Outside is one kind of life, inside is another. And you make them the*
> *same if you lose your hate of prison.* (263)

One of the ways in which Piri copes with prison life is by disavowing any possibility of a "prison culture." As he says, prison is a lie. Any involvement in the
culture of prison not related to "rehabilitation," such as inmates marrying one
another, is a threat to his status as a singular representation of masculinity within
prison. He believes that a hatred for prison life and, by extension, other inmates
who have in one way or another embraced prison culture is the only way to survive with his masculinity intact. This is another example of Ortiz's "necessary
exclusion" of "counter-revolutionaries," in this case, participants in prison culture. Ironically, Piri's "revolution" in this case is predicated on release on good
behavior and a genuine attempt at what he and the parole board deem "rehabilitation." Those prison inmates who are there for life, without possibility of parole, have refused this proscribed rehabilitative path, rejected "outside" culture
and instead generated new culture and possibilities within prison. Piri might
have found more possibility for individualism with these people, or with the
practitioners of radical Islam who attempt to get him to join the Brotherhood.
They seem to come the closest to offering him an explanation for his liminal position, but he rejects them in favor of a "white God" because he knows that that
God is the only one that will lead him to salvation from prison life. Again, Piri is
faced with what he sees as an unpalatable path that requires him to surrender
part of his self in order to become empowered as part of a larger We ("outside")
and chooses it because it remakes him as a "new man." When he is informed of
his successful parole, he tells one of his friends in prison, Big Turk, who tells
him

> Dig, man, you've been re-ha-bi-li-tated, like, uh, you're a changed cat, a
> credit to the human race.
>   I smiled at him and thought, *Jesus, buddy, you don't know how*
> *right you are. I ain't ever gonna be the same. I'm changed all right.* (306)

Echoing Jim's prayer on Ricardo's behalf, Piri invokes the same higher power to
express his happiness at his total transformation. Now that he has finally and
completely abjected the person he used to be (he will never "be the same") he
can become the man he now knows he always wanted to be.

Piri's position within the middle capitalism of the United States in the early twentieth century is a result of, most immediately, his class status and skin color. This is where I believe these texts cross the borders, or rather intersections, of blackness, disability, and latinidad. Ricardo, I have argued, represents a strong resistance to the colonizing impulse to "save" an (individual who has been imagined as) immigrant from a particular kind of deviance but also, though perhaps less directly, from HIV/AIDS. The disproportionate impact of this disease (as well as many other disabling conditions) on persons of color populations suggests a reason why the oppression of Ricardo can be read broadly and thematically across boundaries of race, color, and sexuality. Crucially, Piri expresses a resistance to a particular deployment of "blackness" that *erases* these boundaries entirely and substitutes the binary of "black or white." Together, Pipi and Ricardo's stories demonstrate a "border-consciousness" that visualizes ways through and around the border without resorting to a denial of its very real and often painful existence.

Piri's resistance, however, is mediated by his limited ability to critique his situation through anything other than capitalist logic – that is to say, he lacks the ability to "see again" why he is where he is. This is not to say that he does not frequently and incisively criticize these mechanisms of power and empire, as he certainly understands the absurdity of the racist hegemony of the United States, but he fails in that this hegemony succeeds in ultimately indoctrinating him in the cold logic of the American empire. He has been convinced that all his failures are his own and his successes are also failures. For him, the "one true path" to salvation has been found – it is only after the transformation effected by the disciplinary state that he truly understands the error of his ways and can begin to repent. I have said before that the "failure" of this text and *The Transformation* is supposed to be located in the subjects of the texts, but in reality can be read as a failure to fully indoctrinate the subjects; that is to say, they have failed to become normative subjects. In Piri's case, it is clear that he has become indoctrinated, but the tone of the text seems to enable another reading: that Piri is, like Winston Smith in Orwell's *1984*, both a willing and unwilling subject of state power. While the "success" of the state is total within the structure of the book, our awareness of and exteriority to the narrative reverse that success and refashion the text into a type of bellwether of dystopic possibilities.

"Speaks of my existence"

Sara, Gina, Gigi, and the others lived in and gave a name to "the salt mines," the garbage dump where the city of New York stored raw sodium chloride for deicing roads in the winter, so the products of the market can continue to move about freely in the face of severe weather. The people living there seem to be subsumed into that same construction, into a "biopolitics of disposability" (Giroux 175). Invisible until needed, the two alternatively useful and wasteful (by)products of the state inhabit the same space. This is a borderlands, and it is a space that the abjection of other "selves" requires not exist. That is to say, Ricardo and Piri's success depends on the abjection of their "past" selves, and the rejection of multiple identities, or, an identity that is not intelligible in the logic of the systems they inhabit. The rhetoric of transformation ignores the reality of the mixed consciousness Piri/Piri and Ricardo/Sara must have, "confess" to having. In the preface to *Borderlands/La Frontera*, Anzaldua explains the difficulties and rewards of the border:

> It's not a comfortable territory to live in, this place of contradictions. Hatred, anger, and exploitation are the prominent features of this landscape. [...] Living on borders and in margins, keeping intact one's shifting and multiple identity and integrity, is like trying to swim in a new element, an "alien" element. [...] This book, then, speaks of my existence. (19)

The abjection of these alternate, "past" identities is nothing less than a rejection of the *possibility* of a border subject. To accept the border would be to undermine the logic of transformation – that it is both necessary and permanent, and that one is "better off" afterwards.

If the church and the fundamentalists plant themselves firmly on one side of the border, the side of the proper, heteronormative American dream, then Giovanna's position is much more complex, and at the same time, simpler. Although we see her basically very happy and satisfied life in *The Transformation*, a scene from an earlier documentary called *The Salt Mines* (1990) is spliced in as a kind of "before and after" for Giovanna:

> I don't have no American dream. My dream is my dream. It is not an American dream. And I feel very strongly about that. My dream is my dream and it's not American. And my dream – what is my dream? To one day have a job and a home that I can go to, to be looked and to be treated like a regular human being. That simple. It's not too much to ask for, is it?

Sara, before she becomes Ricardo, has a similar opinion on the "American dream":

> I am from Cuba. [...] My name is Ricardo, my nickname, Sara. I was in jail in Cuba before I came to the United States. For me the U.S. was the most beautiful country on earth, I couldn't wait to come. But now I'm sorry I came, because here, if you have no money you are nothing.

Giovanna's feelings could be called dis-identification and Sara's disillusionment, but they are both critiquing the signification of wealth, prosperity, and happiness around "America" in the immigrant imagination. A case could be made, though, that at this point in history, it is much more located within the already "American" imagination than in the immigrant imagination. These American institutions of capitalism, justice, religion, and white heteronormativity imagine themselves to be rehabilitative and transformative, but the terms of such a transformation make it impossible and fatal. In this sense, we can see Sara and Piri's stories as oddly hopeful narratives of ways of living that are never entirely subsumed into the mechanisms of empire. Instead, those who succeed in resisting transformation are constructed outside the system, on the margins or the border, in a third-space where "identity" is no longer limited and proscribed, but generative and chosen.

---

[1] I insist on this point not only to underscore the logical and linguistic fallacies of the ministry that are skewered so effectively by Sara's very existence, but to stake the claim that the variety and malleability of sexual desires and configurations is much more broadly known even within the ministry and the confines of the film. This is especially apparent during Betty's too-brief discussion of her own sexuality apart from Ricardo's.

[2] Violence is a constant theme throughout *Down These Mean Streets*, especially violent acts committed by Piri to "prove himself" to other men or to himself, as well as frequent and consequence-free violence against women, by Piri and others to prevent women from "talking back" or intervening in the circular logic of the intertwining of masculinity and righteousness.

Works Cited

The Transformation. Dir. Susana Aikin and Carlos Aparicio. 1996. Frameline
    Distribution, 2005.

Anzaldua, Gloria. *Borderlands/La Frontera*. San Francisco: Aunt Lute Books,
    1987.

Giroux, Henry A. "Reading Hurricane Katrina: Class, Race and the Biopolitics
    of Disposability." *College Literature* 33.3 (2006): 171-96.

McRuer, Robert. *Crip Theory: Cultural Signs of Queerness and Disability*. New
    York: New York UP, 2006.

Ortiz, Ricardo L. "Revolution's Other Histories: The Sexual, Cultural and
    Critical Legacies of Roberto Fernandez Retamar's 'Caliban.'" *Social Text*
    58 (Spring 1999): 33-58.

Thomas, Piri. *Down These Mean Streets*. New York: Random House, 1997.

Warner, Michael. *The Trouble with Normal: Sex, Politics, and the Ethics of
    Queer Life*. Cambridge: Harvard UP, 2000.

Chris Bell

"Could This Happen to You?": Stigma in Representations of the Down Low

On 3 August 2003 the average American retrieved her copy of the venerable *New York Times* from her front doorstep. As she rifled through its pages, she most likely paused at the salacious title of the cover story of that week's issue of the *New York Times Magazine*: "Living (and Dying) on the Down Low: Double lives, AIDS, and the black homosexual underground." Her curiosity piqued, she might have allowed her eyes to linger on the representation accompanying these words: the image of two black men, dressed in baggy clothes, standing a few paces away from each other in a garishly-lit parking lot in Anytown, America. As she read through the article, she might have wagged her head in disbelief over the behaviors of these black men, individuals who are involved in relationships with women, but who frequently engage in sexual dalliances "on the down low," in secret. According to the narrative of the *New York Times Magazine*, this behavior is not just morally corrupt, but also pathological as it exposes "innocent" black women to HIV.

If the average American I have described above shared one thing in common with her fellow citizens having finished this piece that summer Sunday it would undeniably be a sense of anger: anger directed not at the scopophilic representation of non-normative sexuality nor at the almost predictable fashion in which this article demonizes and maligns black men as sexual predators, following a long teleological history of this type of depiction.[1] No, her anger most likely arose as a result of the actions of these men on the down low who could not simply own up to what they are like every other red-blooded American.

This essay provides a historic overview of the term "down low," emphasizing how its usage differs in its origins (hip hop music) and its current application (in the print media). I then turn my attention to a textual analysis of the ways the early twenty-first century frenzy and unrelenting spectacle surrounding the down low played out, drawing particular attention to issues of representation and agency, blame and scapegoating, and the ways that AIDS was (once again) used as a tool of policing desire. Writing in "Cultural Studies and Its Theoretical Legacies," Stuart Hall suggests that "AIDS is a question of who gets represented and who does not" (285). I am extending Hall's argument, applying it to the nexus of not only AIDS representations, but overarching representations of sexual sub-cultures (although AIDS certainly informs and inflects the topic under discussion, as we shall see). By looking at a series of (primarily mainstream) newspaper reports, I examine how these representations are inaugurated and what they signal about our current cultural climate, that is, the way we in America live now. Following Hall, the down low is an invitation to contest who gets represented, how they are represented, and with what investments. But not only that, the down low is as much about misguided and outdated beliefs about race, in particular black male sexuality, as it is about misplaced moral panic about HIV incidence and prevalence.

Although the term "down low" entered popular discourse courtesy of the *Times* article in 2003, the phrase had been a staple in hip-hop culture for some time. In 1994, hip-hop trio TLC released "Creep," the first single from their sophomore album. The narrative of the song turns on the description of a (hetero)sexual dalliance, involving a woman "creeping" around on her male partner. As lead singer T-Boz observes in the chorus: "So I creep (yeah) / Just keep it on the down low / Because nobody is supposed to know." In this instance, "down low" refers to keeping something quiet, secretive, on the lower frequencies. It is not a behavior that immediately gives rise to any non-heterosexual insinuations. Given the fact that "Creep" is the first instance of the phrase "down low" appearing in hip-hop culture, it is important to underscore the song's success: once made available as a single, the song sold two million copies; the song reached the top of the R&B and pop charts; and the album the song is culled from, *CrazySexyCool*, was certified by RIAA, the Recording Industry Association of America, as having sold over ten million copies, which, at the time, made it the best-selling album ever released by a female group.

In 1996,[2] hip-hop artist R. Kelly released his single "Down Low" which experienced the same success as the TLC single in terms of airplay and sales. A remix version of this video was the #1 video on BET's (Black Entertainment Television) top 100 year-end countdown. The video features Kelly in the role of bodyguard to Lila Hart, a mobster's girlfriend. Kelly's character and Hart fall in love but agree that it would be better to keep their relationship on the down low lest they incur the wrath of Mr. Big, the mobster. No stranger to over-the-top melodrama,[3] Kelly included enough elements of pathos and (perhaps unintentional) bathos to make song and video linger in the consciousness. Even today, both "Creep" and "Down Low" are recurrent on urban and pop radio stations and video outlets. Thus, the term "down low" is a linguistic phrase that began in hip-hop culture. The phrase implied secrecy and had nothing to do with non-heteronormative activity.

In much the same way that the alternative queer paper the *New York Native* scooped the mainstream press with its early reportage of the AIDS crisis, a minor newspaper beat the mighty *New York Times* with a reference to the down low in the summer of 2003. *POZ* Magazine, a magazine aimed at HIV-positive individuals, published a special edition that summer. One of the articles is entitled "Undercover Brothers," and opens as such:

> Just as afternoon is waning, you'll find Jamal in a secluded section of Prospect Park, Brooklyn – young and good looking, rocking a navy down coat, baggy jeans and a white do-rag. He's waiting, like the other men idling on the edge of this wooded area, for the sun to go down. After dark, he'll follow them down paths into dense bushes to have anonymous and, in many cases, unprotected sex. But by day, Jamal is in a relationship with a woman with whom he has a 2-year-old daughter. Stacie doesn't know about Jamal's quick trysts in the shadows. (Winter 20)

Although the phrase "down low" is never expressly mentioned in the article, there can be no denying that it is on the mind of the writer. Consider Winter's claim that "Jamal is the personification of a new cultural obsession" (20) and that "For now, men like Jamal, and the women who love them, navigate a wilderness of sexual secrecy, shame and misinformation" (22). Given *POZ*'s limited reach in comparison to the *New York Times*, it is not surprising that public uproar following this article was limited if evident at all. Had these exact same words appeared in the pages of the *Times*, they would have immediately caused raised fears in the heart of mainstream America about unthinking black men willfully killing innocent individuals. But since *POZ*'s readership is those individuals who are already infected with HIV – and, arguably, those who treat these individuals – mainstream America (read uninfected America) could ignore the representation… at least for a few more weeks anyway. If anything, mainstream America could adopt the same attitude as Winter's interview subject, Jamal, and his potential risk for acquiring and/or spreading HIV:

Doesn't Jamal feel responsible for protecting [his girlfriend] from STDs like HIV? "Stacie ain't my wife," Jamal says, without losing his thug cool. "She's my baby mama, and we kick it and shit – but she has to take care of her shit, and I take care of mine." Jamal doesn't know his HIV status and shrugs when asked if he plans to get tested. "Naw, man," he says. "I don't wanna know." (23)

To reiterate, it is one thing when a minor HIV publication touts a new health "crisis" in however unsubstantiated and anecdotal a fashion. It is an entirely different thing when the *New York Times* does so, even if the *Times* article is mired in unsubstantiated claims and tantalizing anecdotes as well. Thus, when the front page article appeared in the *New York Times Magazine* on 3 August 2003, it singlehandedly created and sustained the first twenty-first-century frenzy about black male bodies.[4] To wit, this was the first time that the *Times Magazine* featured non-heterosexual black men on its cover and the article itself is so steeped in demonization, marginalization, and scare tactics that it is a wonder that it received an editor's imprimatur.

The first impression[5] one receives having read through the *Times* article is that the *New York Times* simply does not know what to do with these men. They are half-celebrated for their ability to blaze their own path while simultaneously being half-denigrated for not conforming to societal norms and standards. Moreover, there does not seem to be much of an attempt made to make sense of this subculture. A case in point is the notion of unsuspecting wives and girlfriends which is constantly recycled throughout the article for no particular reason. Arguably, the idea is to illuminate a connection between the down low and AIDS but – and herein lies the rub – very little statistical evidence is offered to support this claim.

In lieu of actual evidence, there is posturing, speculation, and a decided insistence on reading the down low men through the lens of psychosocial models of identity development. In the first instance, Denizet-Lewis makes an unveiled appeal to the reader, letting us know that he is a trustworthy narrator. While conducting undercover research at a gay bathhouse in Cleveland, Ohio, Denizet-Lewis is approached by an individual named Flex who makes no secret of the fact that he is attracted to Denizet-Lewis. As the two engage in conversation, clad only in towels as Denizet-Lewis informs us, Flex propositions him (30). Denizet-Lewis declines. The declination could have occurred for myriad reasons; nonetheless, I think it is important for Denizet-Lewis to ward off the advance, lest the reader think that bias is in evidence.

Equally problematic is the way that Denizet-Lewis insists on speculating about the down low men's sexuality. Recall the subtitle of the article: "Double lives, AIDS and the black homosexual underground." None of these men would consider themselves "homosexual," yet that does not stop them from being depicted as such. In a similar fashion, the article's tagline alludes to an unflinching desire to apply Eriksonian models of identity development to these down low individuals:

> To their wives and colleagues, they're straight.
> To the men they have sex with, they're forging an exuberant new identity.
> To the gay world, they're kidding themselves.
> To health officials, they're spreading AIDS throughout the black community. (28)

The discourse is fascinating: "forging an exuberant new identity" to describe what has been alternately referred to as "creeping" (recall TLC) or "having an affair" (recall the many narratives of this behavior over the past several centuries) is undeniable hyperbole. Yet Denizet-Lewis gets away with it. The reader should note as well Denizet-Lewis's formulation of "the gay world" which would appear to be a code phrase or signifier for "the white gay world," as well as his idea of a singular, structuralist "black community" where, evidently, tens of millions of different individuals are able to find common (political) ground based solely on their experience of race.

In "The Culture Industry: Enlightenment as Mass Deception," Max Horkheimer and Theodor Adorno argue that living in a culture that lays claims to, and heralds, certain ideals over others is an immediate invitation to marginalize and subjugate those who do not subscribe to those ideals. Those individuals who do not act "properly" and/or comport themselves according to the bare minimum of societal standards are, in Horkheimer and Adorno's conceptualization, "left behind." The down low is a clear instantiation of this although prior to leaving these down low individuals behind, the *New York Times* aims to expose them in all of their shame, to stigmatize them. As previously indicated, the article would not smart as much as it does if it were (1) able to convincingly trace a link between down low behavior and the spread of AIDS throughout the "entire black community"; (2) not so reliant on reading black male sexuality through an epistemology of the closet; and (3) not wedded to an exclusionary discourse that fails to take into account that down low behavior is not limited to black men.[6]

Two weeks after the article initially appeared, the *Times* printed a series of letters in response. The vast majority took issue with the *Times*'s reportage for the reasons I've enumerated above. For my purposes, I find one letter in particular of importance. The author, Philip B. Spivey of New York, writes:

> I have worked with men of all races and from all walks of life in a clinical setting for more than 20 years and have seen a wide spectrum of sexual orientations and behavior. I came away from your article dismayed and saddened. What was the purpose of this report? To build compassion and understanding for a marginalized group within a marginalized group? To suggest new avenues of public policy for H.I.V. prevention in a population decimated by H.I.V.? I think not. Rather, it seems to me that your treatment of poor and working-class bisexual black men only sensationalizes, demonizes and further marginalizes. One way to rectify this lopsided picture would be to give the lowdown on middle- and upper-class bisexual white men who are married and who frequently tryst with their boy toys.

Spivey encapsulates much of the frustration of the other letter writers, and, perhaps unbeknownst to him, a portion of his letter – the phrase "marginalized group within a marginalized group" – gestures towards a chief concern in intersectionality theory. "In Black (W)holes and the Geometry of Black Female Sexuality," black feminist critic Evelynn Hammonds asserts, "visibility in and of itself does not erase a history of silence nor does it challenge the structure of power ad domination, symbolic and material, that determines what can and cannot be seen" (141). This statement has resonance not only insofar as the down low but for the overarching spectrum of queer and/or non-normative sexualities. As I argue momentarily, the year 2003 was a breakthrough year for queer culture. It would be erroneous, though, to presume that there are not divisions within queer culture, divisions based primarily on race and class (as Spivey glosses above). Accordingly, while some individuals and communities can revel in the power, privilege and authority that comes from newfound or newly-granted cultural dispensation, other individuals and communities are striving to acquire a piece of the cultural pie or, drawing on the title of Bruce Bawer's controversial text, a place at the table.

What the *Times* article illuminates, intentionally or not, is the multivalent nature of queer and non-normative sexualities. It is one thing, for example to be a wealthy white Congressman and be charged with soliciting for sex. This does not necessarily have to curtail one's career (as was the case with Representative Barney Frank who, early in his congressional career, had this charge leveled at him). It is an entirely different thing to be a young, black, relatively powerless subject and have the *New York Times* descend on you in purporting to represent you and what you do. Individuals with cultural cachet and dispensation, like Frank, can draw on their resources to deflect and defend (if not outright dismiss) inaccurate representations. Individuals like the down low men can have writers like Spivey come to their aid but only if the *Times* agrees to publish the letters. Furthermore, publishing a brief letter offering a counternarrative is not guarantee that the collective mindsets of Americans will reevaluate the stance, tone, and content of the article. In the case of the down low, once it's in print, it becomes historic fact.

This is not to suggest that there were not additional attempts to defuse and destabilize the *Times*'s depiction of the down low. From late 2002 until late 2007, black gay activist Keith Boykin maintained a website offering daily updates on depictions of black male sexuality. The day after the publication of the Times article, Boykin filed a column on his site entitled "The Big Down Low Lie." He observes:

Where was the media coverage when black men were having sex with men on the down low and black women weren't getting infected with HIV? Where was the media coverage when black gay and bisexual men were dying of AIDS by the thousands in the 80s and 90s? Why didn't the media care about AIDS when they were dying? And why are black men's lives not worth covering unless we're supposedly killing somebody else? [...] It's time to stop blaming other people and start accepting personal responsibility for the spreading of HIV. If you become positive after willingly having unprotected, nonprocreative sex and you decide to blame your partner, then you probably want to sue McDonald's for making you fat too. Sure the French fries aren't healthy, but you knew that when you ate them. [...] AIDS is a huge problem in our community. It doesn't matter how we got here, we're here. It doesn't matter how anyone got it, they have it. It doesn't matter who's to blame. It matters how we respond to it. The big lie of the down low is not just the lie men tell their women. No, the big lie is the lie we tell ourselves – that it's somebody else's responsibility.

Although I find it problematic that Boykin buys into the false rhetoric of a singular, structuralist black community that Denizet-Lewis also gives so much purchase to in the *Times* article, I value Boykin's critique for drawing on logic as well as his decision not to mince words. What the *Times* article – as well as overarching discourse about the down low – does is cast aspersions on an already subjugated faction of American culture. In that sense, it is a rather Machiavellian narrative, what with its depiction of a powerless cultural segment by an immensely hegemonic cultural entity.

If the *New York Times*, as this immensely hegemonic cultural entity, has a competitor in the world of media representation, it would be the *Washington Post*.[7] For this reason, it is not much of a coincidence that the same day the *Times* ran its article, the *Post* ran a cover story about men on the down low. The focus of the article was quite different though. In lieu of depicting the salacious behavior of the men, the author, Jose Antonio Vargas, played up the ostensible effects of the men's behavior on the women in their lives. This is made clear at the outset in the title of the article, particularly the subtitle: "HIV-Positive, Without A Clue: Black Men's Hidden Sex Lives *Imperiling Female Partners*" (emphasis mine). Indeed, Vargas's entire slant throughout the article is that the women lack the agency to ask the men in their lives some very basic questions about sexual health. The women are innocent; the men are guilty. The women are doing everything right and proper; the men are acting deceitfully. The women are "innocent victims"; the men are predatory brutes.

Vargas's article opens as such:

> She tested positive for HIV in October, infected by the man she had married the year before. He hadn't told her that he was HIV-positive and that he slept with men. She got pregnant. They got married. And, at 26 months old, their daughter died from HIV complications. "If only he told me he preferred men over women. If only he came out with it. We could have been just friends. [...] I'm very angry, I'm very hurt. ... This is someone who killed my child. ... I want revenge. I mean, I've wanted revenge. ... Should I kill him? Sue him?" She collects herself, and with half a smile edging back onto her face, she asks, "What can women do?"

It is difficult to criticize this characterization without appearing to "blame the victim." Nonetheless, it is important to call into question the women's agency and responsibility to protect themselves. The entire burden of communication is placed on the men in this narrative. While it would have been helpful if the men had disclosed their seropositive status, it might also have been helpful if the women had asked pointed questions and sought honest responses. If, drawing on a safer sex mantra from the 1990s, protection is the priority, then the responsibility – and failure – to secure protection must be shared equally amongst partners. The interview subject's interrogatory of "What can women (plural) do?" must be problematized because it longs to pit black women against black men in much the same way the Moynihan Report did in the 1960s.

In much the same way that the *New York Times* demonstrated that it did not know what to do with men on the down low, so too has American culture manifested a profound disinclination to allow such behavior to go uncommented on. The down low gives rise to all sorts of unfounded and unsubstantiated moral panic from a public as well as a bureaucratic perspective (a case in point in the latter vein is the Centers for Disease Control and Prevention's addition of "men on the down low" as a category of risk of transmission of HIV as well as its swift removal of the same shortly thereafter once the agency was challenged by black gay activists to show evidence that this risk group actually leads to increased infections and transmission). Even from a sociolinguistic perspective, the frenzy about the down low has given rise to what Jose Munoz has termed disidentification: as I explained earlier in this chapter, the phrase down low originated in hip-hop culture to mark a sexual dalliance. Recently, it appears that hip hop culture – which has always maintained a fraught relationship with issues of queerness and masculinity – has followed the mindset of mainstream America in distancing itself from the subversive resonances the down low gives rise to. Consider the recent collaboration between hip-hop impresario P. Diddy and his protégé Mario Winans, "I Don't Wanna Know" (2004), in which Winans suspects his partner might be cheating on him: "I don't wanna know / If you're playing me / Keep it on the low." To emphasize, Winans does not state "Keep it on the *down* low," despite the fact that doing so does not throw off the measure of the lyric. I contend that "the low" is the new, uncomplicated (read: not inclined to tie the subject in with predators) way of referencing the down low. "The low" is a sanitized version of "creepin'"; the "down low" has become irreparably tainted.[8]

The fact that the down low is an incentive for America to take a reflexive look at itself – namely, the way it represents the "other" – is undeniable. What must be clarified is the way this gazing occurs e.g., from whence it hails. It is all too easy, although not entirely incorrect, to list the down low as merely another instantiation of America's centuries-long emasculation of black men. It is more difficult, and thereby crucially important, to note the ways that the down low encourage the monolithic construct of "the black community" to take a look at itself. In "Black Macho Revisited: Reflections of a SNAP! Queen," cultural critic Marlon Riggs practically predicts the down low in his assessment of disidentification within "the black community":

> What lies at the heart, I believe, of black America's pervasive cultural homophobia is the desperate need for a convenient Other *within* the community, yet not truly *of* the community, an Other to which blame for the chronic identity crises afflicting the black male psyche can be readily displaced, an indispensable Other which functions as the lowest common denominator of the abject, the base line of transgression beyond which a Black Man is no longer a man, no longer black, an essential Other against which black men and boys maturing, struggling with self-doubt, anxiety, feelings of political, economic, social, and sexual inadequacy – even impotence – can always measure themselves and by comparison seem strong, adept, empowered, superior. (152-53; emphasis in original)

In *The Boundaries of Blackness: AIDS and the Breakdown of Black Politics*, political scientist Cathy Cohen describes the politics of secondary marginalization within "the black community," underscoring how marginalized individuals with privilege (in the instance of the down low, the hegemonic privilege of heterosexuality and/or monogamy) police those without privilege.

It would be disingenuous not to comment on the claim that the *New York Times* article specifically – as well as other articles about the down low including the *Washington Post* article – had to be written by a non-black individual. Folklorists have commented on the reticence to "air dirty laundry" in black communities, an idea which implies that even in times of great communal crisis and strain, it is best to keep a stiff upper lip and soldier forth in the face of hegemonic white observation and oppression. The consequences of not doing so can be dire as observed when law professor Anita Hill "dared" to challenge her former boss, Clarence Thomas, who had been nominated to the US Supreme Court. Writing in "Race, Sex, and Indifference" (153-54), Carole Pateman argues – as many black feminist critics did in 1991 and the years immediately following – that Hill lost the support of the "black community" because she opted to see herself as a woman first instead of privileging her race over her sex:

The complexities of the position of black women, and the corrosive effects of the sexual and racial contracts, were highlighted when Anita Hill, a former employee of Clarence Thomas at the Equal Employment Opportunity Commission, accused him of sexual harassment during his nomination for the Supreme Court. The hearings of the Senate Judiciary Committee became a major public spectacle after Hill's accusation. The Chair of the Committee ruled that the burden of proof lay with Hill, and the Senators apparently found it difficult to believe that sexual harassment was commonplace in workplaces. The hearings and media coverage turned not on Thomas's conduct but on Hill's truthfulness, another episode in the very long history of distrust in women's ability to tell the truth combined with an even greater disbelief in black women's veracity. Many African Americans saw the charge of sexual harassment as part of a white feminist agenda that operated to the detriment of black men and so as casting doubt on Hill (Burnham 1992: 311-13). They also saw Hill as violating a code in her own community. She had criticized a fellow African American in public and raised the question of the treatment of black women by black men. The breach, Hill said, "damned me in the eyes of many Blacks whose profound experiences of racism have led them to ignore within our own community what we find intolerable when committed by others against us" (A. Hill 1995: 284).

Thus, there is some credence to be given to the argument that only a non-black individual could have written the *Times* piece since a black individual would have been committing communal suicide in doing so.

This does not however explain the inherent double standard of the down low. In 2004, the governor of New Jersey resigned over allegations that he had engaged in a same-sex affair while in office. In reporting this – as well as the account of his divorce from his wife – neither the *New York Times* nor other media outlets referred to him as being on the down low. Clearly, the governor's racial status (white) prevented him (read: protected him) from being conceived as such.[9] In 2005, audiences across the world turned out in droves to view the film *Brokeback Mountain* which tells the story of Jack Twist and Ennis del Mar, two married ranchers who engage in a nineteen-year relationship with one another. Few audience members and/or critics applied the appellation "down low" to this behavior, revealing the double standard that is a constitutive element of the "phenomenon": when black men are on the down low, it's a moral crisis; when white men are on the down low, or more to the point, portray men on the down low, they are nominated for Oscars.

[1] I offer Emmitt Till and Michael Jackson, and Gus in D. W. Griffith's fictional *Birth of a Nation* (1915), as instructive examples.

[2] Between "Creep" (1994) and "Down Low" (1996), adult contemporary artist Brian McKnight released a single entitled "On the Down Low" in 1995. The song was only a minor hit on the R&B chart and did not register at all on the pop chart. I include it here to demonstrate how the phrase "down low" was in circulation on radio (primarily urban outlets) and TV (primarily MTV, BET, and VH1) throughout the mid-1990s, with its usage having little to do with non-heteronormative behavior.

[3] The reader should recall Kelly's (in)famous "Trapped in the Closet" saga (2005) which features twenty installments of Rufus, his wife, and the steadily-increasing number of individuals, male and female, that they engage in sexual activity with.

[4] Interestingly, in early 2003, *Times* reporter Jayson Blair was fired from his staff position after it was revealed that he had never interviewed some of the sources that he utilized in his articles and that others were completely fabricated. This firing set off a period of ethical soul-searching in American journalism with Blair offering a *mea culpa* for his actions. His doing so, I contend, was the only reason that his race (black) did not figure into the discourse more than it did. Being one of only a handful of reporters of color at America's most respected newspaper would obviously place a person under performance pressure. Both Blair and the *Times* were careful not to demonize all reporters of color generally and black reporters specifically for Blair's actions. For this reason, I do not consider the Blair episode as "creating and sustaining the first twenty-first-century frenzy about a black male body." It seemed evident that both parties just wished the attention would go away. That was not the case with the down low.

[5] I should mention that ten months before this article was published, I was contacted by its writer, Benoit Denizet-Lewis. He had learned of the work I was engaged in at the time in HIV/AIDS prevention and education, work which primarily involved me speaking to high school and college-aged audiences about risk factors, protection, and overall sexual health. We spoke via phone for three hours in Atlanta, Georgia, where I had just concluded a prevention and education program held at the main branch of the Atlanta Public Library. Originally, the sponsoring organization, the Human Rights Campaign, had intended to convene the program on the campus of one of Atlanta's four HBCUs (historically black college and university). However, support was not forthcoming from any of the power-holders at the HBCUs because, as the Vice President of Student Affairs at one of the schools memorably phrased it, "There would be no need to come to this university and talk about gay men and AIDS because there are no gay men here." I relayed this narrative to Denizet-Lewis along with other observations about attitudes towards AIDS in the black community. Indeed, when Denizet-Lewis initially broached the subject of the *Times* article with me, it was pitched as a comprehensive story about "AIDS in the black community." Although we spoke about the down low, and portions of my comments about the down low appear in the *Times* article, I was not under the impression that the entire article would be down low-focused. Given the circumstances surrounding Jayson Blair and the attendant ethical soul-searching I referenced above, I wonder how many other individuals Denizet-Lewis interviewed under false pretenses.

[6] The reader should recall, for instance, Plato's *Symposium* which depicts Socrates pining for young Alcibiades while Xanthippe, Socrates' wife, waits at home. The point is not a minor one: the down low frenzy has historical antecedents that had never been explored in this capacity prior to 3 August 2003. To deny the extra-marital dalliances frequently engaged in by non-black individuals, to limit the scope of cheating to one racialized subject, is specious.

[7] Katharine Graham's Pulitzer Prize-winning *Personal History* analyzes the historic rivalry between these two news outfits.

[8] The same year that the Winans's song hit the top of the pop and R&B charts, pop thrush Beyoncé released "Me, Myself and I," the third single from her debut album. Drawing on this idea of "the low" as the new sanitized version of the down low, it is noteworthy that in the second verse of the song, in which Beyoncé gives a wayward suitor his walking papers, she offers evidence that "Even your very best friend / Tried to warn me / On the low."

[9] In 2005, Governor McGreevey and his wife Dana appeared on *Oprah*. At no point during the hour-long episode did the talk show host utter the phrase "down low." A few weeks later when author Terry McMillan and her estranged husband Jonathan Plummer appeared on the show to discuss Plummer's extra-marital affairs with men, Winfrey pointedly posited, "So, you're on the down low." This was more of a descriptive statement than a question, which would explain why Winfrey then turned to face the audience/cameras directly, to provide a description of what the down low is.

Works Cited

Beyoncé. "Me, Myself and I." *Dangerously In Love*. Columbia, 2004.

Boykin, Keith. "The Big Down Low Lie." *keithboykin.com* 4 Aug. 2003. N. d. <http://www.keithboykin.com/arch/2003_08_04.html>.

Denizet-Lewis, Benoit. "Double Lives on the Down Low." *The New York Times Magazine* 3 Aug. 2003. 28-33, 48, 52-53.

Hall, Stuart. "Cultural Studies and Its Theoretical Legacies." *Cultural Studies*. Ed. Lawrence Grossberg, Cary Nelson, and Paula Treichler. New York: Routledge, 1992. 277-86.

Hammonds, Evelynn. "Black (W)holes and the Geometry of Black Female Sexuality." *differences* 6. 2-3 (1994): 126-45.

Horkheimer, Max, and Theodor Adorno. "The Culture Industry: Enlightenment as Mass Deception." 1944. *The Dialectic of Enlightenment*. Trans. John Cunning. New York: Continuum, 1993. 120-66.

Pateman, Carole. "Race, Sex, and Indifference." *Contract and Domination*. Ed. Carole Pateman and Charles W. Mills. Cambridge: Polity. 2007. 134-64.

Riggs, Marlon. "Black Macho Revisited: Reflections of a SNAP! Queen." 1991. *Freedom in This Village: Twenty-Five Years of Black Gay Men's Writing*. Ed. E. Lynn Harris. New York: Carrol & Graf, 2004.

Spivey, Phillip B. "Double Lives on the Down Low." *The New York Times Magazine: Letters to the Editor* 17 Aug. 2003. N. d. <http://www.nytimes.com/2003/08/17/magazine/17LETTERS.html>.

TLC. "Creep." *CrazySexyCool*. LaFace Records, 1994.

Winans, Mario, and P. Diddy. "I Don't Wanna Know." *Hurt No More*. Bad Boy, 2004.

Winter, Stephen. "Undercover Brothers." Spec. ed. of *POZ*, 2003. 20-23.

Vargas, Jose Antonio. "HIV-Positive, Without a Clue: Black Men's Hidden Sex Lives Imperiling Female Partners." *The Washington Post* 3 Aug. 2003. N. d. <http://www.washingtonpost.com/ac2/wp-dyn/A16957-2003Aug3>.

Moya Bailey

"The Illest": Disability as Metaphor in Hip Hop Music

> In this context, there's no disrespect, so when I bust my rhyme, you break your necks.
> We got five minutes for us to disconnect, from all intellect and let the rhythm effect
> 'Bout to lose our inhibition. Follow your intuition. Free your inner-soul and break away from tradition.
> (will.i.am, "Let's Get Retarded" / "Let's Get It Started")

In 2003, the hip hop group the Black Eyed Peas released their third album *Elephunk* which featured the controversial track "Let's Get Retarded" (I. Am). The radio edit became "Let's Get It Started" with only a few minor changes made to the verses ("cuckoo" becomes "wohoo"). The repackaged song went on to be featured in several movie soundtracks along with being played at the 2004 Democratic National Convention and was one of the top 100 Pop songs of the year on Billboard's Hot 100 Chart (Newman). The ARC Organization, formerly the Association of Retarded Citizens, successfully lobbied the Pea's record company arguing that the ubiquitous use of the word "retarded" is offensive and damaging to those who are medically labeled with the term (Beckham). Others felt this was an example of the politically correct language police gone too far. I'd like to offer an alternative reading through a *disidentification* with the lyrics as either bad or of little consequence. Words have extreme power and it seems that the persuasive but yet uninvestigated proliferation of ableist language in hip hop begs further exploration. What work are lyrics like "let's get retarded" doing and for whose interests? Drawing largely on the intersectional analysis of Jose Muñoz, I will demonstrate the synergistic properties of looking at this language through multiple lenses at once as a way to forestall the limitations of a binary of good and bad, political correctness and the protected right to free speech.

As I have begun to conceptualize my own research project, I am very aware of the tension between the socially constructed nature of identity and the political impetus to use identity to make claims for adequate and equal treatment in society. I am also interested in how the policing of identity through stigma management impacts the ability of various groups to build coalitions and alliances for advocacy. Do these alternate connotations of ableist language open up or foreclose these possibilities? What follows is a short investigation of these queries.

Jose Muñoz's concept of disidentification is really useful in thinking about people who inhabit the liminal spaces of marginalized categories by virtue of identifying with more than one minority classification of embodiment (Muñoz). As the classic Gloria Hull et al. title advances, *All the Women Are White, All the Blacks Are Men, But Some of Us Are Brave*, existing within the margins of the margins can produce a unique and valuable theoretical perspective (Hull, Scott, and Smith). One is both inside and outside the already marginalized categories black and woman but the combination can create a standpoint that demonstrates the limitations of monolithic constructions of a particular form of marginalization. Minoritarian discourses generated by these multiply marginal subjects offer so much in our attempts to theorize the body as it interacts with the world around it.

By examining ableism in hip hop through the multiple lenses of disability, queer, critical race, and feminist theories we can go beyond the ineffective dichotomy of positive and negative representation and possibly discover useful theorizing derived outside the insulated world of academe. Ableism is the system of oppression that privileges able-bodied people and culture over and above those with disabilities. In the liminal spaces of hip hop the reappropriation of ableist language can mark a new way of using words that departs from generally accepted disparaging connotations. Though this project makes a case for a transgressive reading of ableism in hip hop, ableism in and of itself is still oppressive. Additionally, not all of it can be reimagined. Some of it is simply the vile invective that maintains hierarchies of oppression through able bodied privilege. Though other genres of music and popular culture generally reinforce ableism (Pop Music's love of "crazy" love), its presence in hip hop speaks, I argue, to centuries-old stigma management strategies of politics of respectability that remain futile.

Hip hop was born in 1970's New York City. The East Coast was the original home and as such became the dominant voice of hip hop (Kitwana). The emergence of the laid back yet violent rap sound of California made for the creation of a legendary and ultimately deadly east/west rivalry. This unfortunate history made way for the contemporary moment in which the "Diirty" South rules the landscape with its feel good club bangers. This constant reorientation allows for the emergence of different sounds. The Midwestern, i.e., Chicago sound and the newer, less violent sounds of the Bay Area and LA offer music that has been allowed to develop out of the mainstream's controlling gaze. The California derived sound of The Hyphy Movement's reappropriation of the derisive terms "retarded," "dumb," and LA Krump's dance styling both achieved their transgressive potential through their initial marginalization by mainstream hip hop.

The Bay, or Yay Area as it is sometimes known, along with Los Angeles, has been off the radar of the mainstream hip hop scene for a little over a decade. With the yet unsolved murder of the rapper 2Pac and the escalating violence associated with the genre, so called California "gangsta rap" retreated from the popular scene. New art forms have developed most notably the hyphy sound and krumping dance style, with both making explicit claims to the importance of their regional location and histories of violence as major propellants of the styles.

Getting hyphy, characterized by exaggeration, overness, and overall extraness, offers opportunities for folks to let loose and get loose on the dance floor. Hyphy is also associated with "crazy" behavior like driving with no one behind the wheel with the car doors open or sitting on top of the car while it's moving ("ghost riding the whip"). The addition of whistle tips, a modified metal pate welded to the car's exhaust that makes a high pitched screeching sound, further demonstrates the need to be seen and heard within the hyphy movement.

The social embrace of these ostensibly stigmatizing activities and performances are celebrated for their intentional transgressive power. By actively flouting societal conventions of quiet and sane behavior, black people connected to Hyphy music are challenging their marginalization in a culture that otherwise renders them invisible. They demand attention; even incurring the derision associated with ableism rather than be ignored.

> Sitting in my scraper, watching Oakland go wild... Ta-dow
> I don't bump mainstream, I knock underground
> All that other shit, sugar-coated and watered down

> I'm from the Bay where we hyphy and go dumb
> From the soil where them rappers be getting their lingo. (E-40)

In "Tell Me When to Go," hyphy originator and most recognizable hyphy artist E-40 explains the unique and non-normative nature of the genre by connecting it to the location, as well as pointing out the appropriation of the language by rappers outside the Area. "Going dumb" is marked regionally as being something uniquely produced in California. The violence of California gang activity has been implicated in the production of this alternative culture.

The documentary *Rize* follows the practitioners of krumping from its origins in LA children's clowning parties to a dance form that has reached mainstream audiences through current hip hop choreography (LaChapelle et al.). Though beginning with Tommy the Hip Hop Clown's solo birthday performances, it quickly evolved to dance-battling clown troupes that served as alternatives to gangs for kids in the neighborhoods. As dancers got older the style continued to morph and the even more outrageous krumping was born.

To those unfamiliar, krumping looks violent with battles between dancers a central component. Krumpers hit each other to get amped up to dance in radically expressive and explosive ways. They connect the dance to African tribal warrior and spiritual rituals yet also invoke an internalized colonial gaze using words like primal, crazy, savage, and raw to characterize the link (LaChapelle et al.). So while celebrated and even exalted as a spiritual practice, it is simultaneously imbued with a primitive and barbarous ferocity that is connected to the loss of control.

We see this reapproprtiation in dance. One of the hall marks of hip hop dance is the ability to look free form and accidental. Dancers are seemingly and often instructed in the music to lose control. This loss of control has been lyrically manifested in the seemingly ableist language of getting retarded and going dumb, though in the context of these songs, this is a good thing. Missy Elliot's 2005 hit featuring Ciara "Lose Control" invokes this sentiment (Elliot). The loss of control the freedom afforded to those who let go, who "wile out" is a momentary escape from the strictures of the everyday. The music itself, alcohol, and weed are used to allow people to slip out of their constraints and boxes and just be. There is an association of freedom with one's ability to go dumb and get hyphy. Ironically this ableist language further circumscribes the lives of those who are assigned these labels outside of the hip hop context. For those ascribed the labels "dumb," "retarded," and "crazy," the libratory nature of embracing these terms does not match their reality.

Dumb connotes a lack of intelligence that stigmatizes people and keeps people from being fully engaged in society. Similarly, those labeled retarded are tracked into special education classrooms and segregated from their peers. These acts of separation reinforce stereotypes about the value of people so labeled in a world that excludes them from formative participation. Crazy also serves to malign those ascribed with images of violent and uncontrollable behavior, in direct contrast to the state sanctioned controlled violence many people within mental health conditions describe experiencing.

The freedom that is expressed through the use of going retarded and dumb has the simultaneous effect of further foreclosing the freedom for those who are ascribed these terms by the medicojuridical system. While this language is a temporary escape for hyphy and hip hop practitioners, it presents many problems for those ascribed and held to these labels in the world. Beyond just being offensive, this ableism perpetuates stigmatization, marginalization, and oppressive structural hierarchies of human difference.

Like many other pejorative terms – lame, gyped, gay, bitch – "retard" and "dumb" have lost their referents, or rather the referent is purportedly discarded. When kids say "that's so gay" or "that's retarded" to mean something is bad or uncool, it is not supposed to reflect on the people who are ascribed those labels. Disability theorists argue that this is not true. These statements do in fact reinforce negative connotations on already marginalized groups effectively reinscribing their liminality and Otherness. Disability Studies, like Women's Studies, illuminates the controlling normate in whose fictitious image we discipline our bodies. Part of the need for ableist language in hip hop is the erstwhile stigma that black bodies incur. In a futile attempt to manage their own societal stigma, black men in hip hop often target other marginalized groups including women, queer people, and people with disabilities. But the critical question is how do we congeal these often falsely differentiated populations into tandem resistance? What coalitions might be formed out of a reformulation of stigma management with an understanding of intersectionality?

Erving Goffman wrote extensively about stigma. Goffman researched the original Greek definition of stigma which meant a physical mark on the body that signaled some kind of moral failing in an individual (Goffman). This set the person apart and discredited him/her within the society. While this marking was a literal branding of the undesirables in ancient Greece (criminals, traitors, slaves, etc.), it has evolved to encompass minority groups whose physical characteristics set them apart from the norm (3). People with disabilities or "abominations of the body" were one of the three types of stigma Goffman identified who departed from the anticipated socially constructed norms of the group (5).

Goffman also described "stigma management" strategies employed by marginalized populations to mitigate their subjugated positioning in society. These techniques were employed by a wide variety of stigmatized groups including criminals, sex workers, racial/ethnic minorities, people with disabilities, etc. (20-23).

The autonomy myth is the undergirding societal assumption that all people are (or should be) independent autonomous beings that must provide for themselves (Fineman). This is indirectly coded as able-bodied white, wealthy, and male. This is what produces societal anxiety about people with disabilities, of color, and women, who are imagined as dependants who weigh on others (i.e., men's) autonomy (34). So many of the stigma management strategies of these marginalized groups center on making sure that they are perceived as important contributing members of society and not a drain on its resources.

People with cognitive disabilities are tangentially located within the broader disability movement that often centers physical impairments. People with physical disabilities may even try to distance themselves from this presumably even more stigma producing categorization. The documentary *Murderball* (2005) highlights wheelchair rugby players whose rough and tumble personas as well as sexual prowess are used to separate themselves from cognitive disabilities (Rubin et al.). Film and television often reinforce this problematic construction through the implementation of stereotypical roles and narratives that make the person with a cognitive disability the butt of a joke. The 2008 controversy over the Ben Stiller comedy *Tropic Thunder* (2008) illustrates this point well. In the film, Stiller plays a "retard" who is an actor who thinks that his real life captured by the local people is part of the filming (Stiller et al.). The film's tag line "once there was a retard" was pulled as a result of protests by various disability rights organizations within the US and abroad.

The blatant use of this offensive language speaks to the invisibility of ableism within popular culture. Disability activists have even taken to using the construction "the R-word" like the use of "the N-word." The n-word though has its own reappropriation story that is also connected to hip hop. But what this parallel structure presupposes is an analogous construction. Is Retard to Nigger what bitch is to queer? Vice versa? Are all of these words only as virulent as the person hurling them as an insult? Is it fundamentally different when someone who may identify with these words reappropriates them?

These questions remain as I continue to investigate the simultaneity of reclamation and reinscription that effect communities in such disparate ways. The seemingly celebratory power of language for one marginalized group impedes on the material reality for another and yet there are those who are multiply marginalized who traverse more than one group at the same time. The work of unpacking language that does not easily fit along the binary of positive and negative must propel our thinking into nonlinear dimensions. We must embrace the challenge of multi-dimensional complexity and uncover new models that can accommodate the contradictions of our language.

Works Cited

Beckham, Beverly. "Let's Not Use Words that Have Power to Wound." *The Boston Globe* 21 Mar. 2007.

E-40. *Tell Me When to Go*. BME, 2006.

Elliot, Missy. *Loose Control*. Atlantic, 2005.

Fineman, Martha Albertson. *The Autonomy Myth: A Theory of Dependency*. New York: New P, 2004.

Goffman, Erving. *Stigma: Notes on the Management of Spoiled Identity*. 1963. New York: Touchstone, 1986.

Hull, Gloria T., Patricia Bell Scott, and Barbara Smith. *All the Women Are White, All the Blacks Are Men, but Some of Us Are Brave: Black Women's Studies*. Old Westbury: Feminist P, 1982.

I. Am, Will. *Let's Get It Started*. A&M, 2003.

Kitwana, Bakari. *The Hip Hop Generation: Young Blacks and the Crisis in African American Culture*. New York: Basic Civitas, 2002.

Rize. Dir. David LaChapelle. Lions Gate Home Entertainment, 2005.

Muñoz, José Esteban. *Disidentifications: Queers of Color and the Performance of Politics, Cultural Studies of the Americas.* Minneapolis: U of Minnesota P, 1999.

Newman, Melinda. "NBA Dribbles with the Peas." *Billboard* 10 Apr. 2004. 11, 14.

Murderball. Dir. Henry Alex Rubin and Dana Adam Shapiro. Thinkfilm, 2005.

Tropic Thunder. Dir. Ben Stiller. Paramount, 2008.

Carlos Clarke Drazen

Both Sides of the Two-Sided Coin: Rehabilitation of Disabled African American Soldiers

Introduction

This chapter cannot neatly offer up a discussion limited to black veterans and disabilities related to their military service during wartime. The subject necessarily involves an examination of the history of the American military, in addition to the history of disability in America, as well as the broader civil rights movement. The histories feed off of each other, and are so intertwined that sometimes unexpected consequences occur and the result of one action becomes the cause of another action. This history, while rich and fascinating, is not easy to put into compartments.

The Civil War

Veterans' benefits have existed in some form since before the Civil War. President Abraham Lincoln officially called for them in his second inaugural address on March 4, 1865. Towards the end of the US Civil War, Lincoln famously called for caring treatment of veterans: "to care for him who shall have borne the battle, and for his widow, and his orphan" (Bredhoff 52). The treatment of black Civil War veterans, however, was decidedly unequal.

> Once the Union government had made the decision in early 1863 to enlist black soldiers, military efficiency and moral arguments demanded that all soldiers, whatever their color, be treated equally. The deep-seated racial prejudice pervasive in American society, however, meant that such a policy faced real resistance. As a result, federal officials moved in hesitant, sometimes ambiguous, but ultimately inevitable steps toward a policy of equal protection and benefits for black soldiers and their families. Nevertheless, social attitudes and conditions meant that even color-neutral legislation had an unequal impact on whites and blacks. (Reid 375)

The government, realizing that they had a responsibility to wounded soldiers and their families, created a pension plan for those who needed it. If the soldier had been killed in battle, or by disease, the pension would go to the widowed family of these men. Not surprisingly, African American veterans were mostly excluded or, in the best case, limited as to "the support offered by various institutions to others involved in the war. The families of black soldiers were slower to receive benefits than the families of white soldiers" (ibid 375-76).

Many black soldiers had joined as slaves and, since slaves could not marry,[1] there was difficulty in proving legitimacy for black families after the war. Thus, access to benefits was difficult if not impossible for surviving family members.

> At the same time, these black families had fewer personal resources to fall back on when the male wage earner was absent, and they were far more vulnerable to harsh retaliation from the society around them. In this, as in many other issues, African Americans experienced a very different Civil War. (Ibid. 376)

African Americans encountered more outright rejections and smaller pension awards than did whites; researchers point to biased pension examiners and documentation rules that were more difficult for black veterans to satisfy than white veterans (Logue and Blank).

Yet African Americans, undaunted by their treatment by the military and the government during and after the Civil War, willingly enlisted in the Army for World War I. The war lasted less than two years for the United States but, in that time, 123,000 disabled soldiers of the American Expeditionary Forces returned from Europe (Bureau of Veterans Affairs). The number was so large that, as in Europe, America had to begin to address the problem of disabled veterans which it had believed up to that point, was not a major concern (Gritzer and Arluke). The question of how to help disabled black veterans was not so much ignored as it was overlooked (Onkst). As in the Civil War, few opportunities were available to disabled black veterans returning from World War I, and fewer benefits.

Rehabilitation of World War I Veterans

In any civilization throughout history, the military has enjoyed a special status. Those who went to war were regarded as heroes; those who returned injured in

battle received special pensions and other benefits. In World War I, these benefits came to include physical rehabilitation.

> Because of the willingness of legislators and their constituents to give ge-
> nerous support to rehabilitation services for veterans it has been possible
> to develop innovations and demonstrations in procedures and techniques
> that could not be attempted in less well endowed programs. Probably only
> by keeping the program for veterans separate fom [sic] slower-moving
> programs was it possible to organize to meet the emergency precipitated
> by the sudden developments related to demobilization following armed
> conflict. However, much has been lost because there has not been an ade-
> quate interchange between those who were administering veterans' reha-
> bilitation and the administrators of rehabilitation activities for nonvete-
> rans. (Obermann 135)

The American government passed legislation for veterans' benefits for virtually
every conflict from the Revolution to the Boxer Rebellion, but "[c]ompensation
and pensions were relied upon to solve the disabled veterans' problems" (ibid.
146).

Just before America entered World War I, the government passed three
federal acts that would bear directly on those disabled in the war: the War Risk
Insurance Act (1914); the Smith-Hughes Act (1917) "to provide for the promo-
tion of vocational education […] in agriculture, the trades, and industry" (ibid.
148), section 6 of which created the Federal Board of Vocational Education; and
the National Defense Act of 1916. Section 37 of the National Defense Act allowed for active duty soldiers to "be given the opportunity to study and receive
instruction upon educational lines" (ibid.) before their return to civilian life. This
reflected a change of attitude, not merely in Congress but nationwide, that realized that the benefits of advanced education could be extended beyond active
servicemen:

> These developing techniques could be applied to disabled persons; that
> disability need not be commensurate with handicap; that residual capabili-
> ties could remain even after severe injury; that these capabilities could be
> discovered and could be developed into vocational effectiveness. (Ibid.
> 149)

After the Armistice, black American troops were demobilized "within
twelve months after the end of the war" (Clement 534). For all practical purpos-

es, this prevented them from taking advantage of Section 37 of the National Defense Act to receive an education.

> The federal government offered no aid to any of these soldiers except to disabled veterans. These men were passed upon by officials of the Veterans Administration, and in many instances had their tuitions and other fees paid at many of the larger universities [...] [R]elatively few Negro ex-soldiers were benefited this way. (Ibid. 535)

The government was more generous with health benefits than educational benefits for black veterans.

> The [Negro] ex-soldier who could prove himself in need of treatment could go to Tuskegee or to one of the other hospitals, and there, without cost, receive excellent medical and hospital services. Soldiers who could prove that they were in ill health because of their war service, but not in need of hospitalization, could be awarded disability compensation which might continue for a term or for the remainder of the soldier's life. [...] It is generally agreed that the Government was more liberal, realistic, and sound in the provisions made for the physical well-being of the ex-soldier than it was in the matter of his return to gainful employment or in the completion of his education. (Ibid. 536)

Clement's positive outlook on health care available to black veterans apparently was not universal. Care was available to those "who could prove that they were in ill health because of their war service"; this became a loophole.

> In examining veterans for service-related disability, physicians routinely applied not medical criteria but cultural and racial values. They regarded certain diseases as prevalent, if not congenital, among particular racial groups. For instance, they considered black Americans biologically predisposed to tuberculosis, despite the absence of clinical studies demonstrating this. Such cultural and racial views of disease, though medical fictions, had real consequences, because in attributing a medical condition to congenital weakness, low standards of personal hygiene, or moral degradation, rather than to military service, physicians invalidated the disability claims of many black veterans. The latter understood this prejudicial logic quite well and objected to it. (Hickel 237)

As with race, social and cultural attitudes on disability tended to get in the way when applied to World War I veterans. There was no consistent definition;

disability was argued over by "employers and employees, skilled and unskilled workers, elected legislators and career bureaucrats, physicians and patients." However, perhaps predictably, "officials reinforced inequities of race and class in administering disability benefits" (ibid. 238).

The selective granting of benefits, amendments to the legislation, added to attrition and aging among the veterans, meant that benefits for World War I veterans were in steady decline throughout the twenties. All vocational education programs were closed out by the summer of 1928 (Obermann 173).

By 1930, military personnel were calling for a veteran's hospital to be located at Tuskegee in Alabama to serve the more than 500,000 Negro veterans in the nation.

> It has been unofficially announced that Dr. Joseph Ward, medical director of the veterans hospital in Alabama, has recommended that the hospital under his direction be made available as a cooperating unit with Tuskegee [...] [T]his constructive move will have a far-reaching effect upon the training of negro doctors and the general health of the negro. ("Ward Want Vets to Unite")

This 600 bed hospital was located within two miles of Tuskegee and the only veterans hospital to treat Negro veterans in the United States.

Planning for World War II

The National Medical Association[2] and the National Colored Graduate Nurses Association agitated for increased black representation; specifically, for the presence of black doctors and nurses, respectively, in the military. These groups struggled throughout World War II to desegregate American military medicine. During the prewar mobilization period, 1940-41, leaders of the National Medical Association (NMA), remembering the segregation of black soldiers and officers during World War I, queried the War Department about their status. In a new war, would black physicians be integrated into the medical corps or relegated to practice in separate facilities (Hine 1281-82)?

Surgeon General James Magee of the U.S. Army answered the question this way:

men who are fulfilling the same obligations, suffering the same dislocation of their private lives, and wearing the identical uniform should, within the confines of the military establishment, have the same privileges of
rest and relaxation that they enjoyed at home. (Qtd. in ibid. 1284)

And, if home observed Jim Crow separation of the races, the military was expected to offer Negro soldiers the same "convenience."

While the black professional organizations and, increasingly, black communities across America were agitating for an end to segregation in the military,
Magee sounded out his peers in the Army. He was told that intelligence tests
"proved" that African Americans were unequipped to handle "technical aspects
of medical care." This perceived inferiority made the War Department wonder if
more than a handful of black doctors were even equipped to serve in the military
(ibid. 1286).

During the summer of 1941, with black medical professionals and the
military at an impasse, militant anger increased in the black community. In that
summer, A. Philip Randolph and the Brotherhood of Sleeping Car Porters (a recently formed black union) called for a march on Washington. This call for
100,000 black people to protest in the nation's capital pushed President Franklin
Roosevelt to sign Executive Order #8802, outlawing discrimination in American
defense industries and establishing the Fair Employment Practices Commission
(ibid. 1287).

Also in 1941, American physicians, scientists, and social scientists were
part of an interdisciplinary team known as the Manhattan Project, which led to
the creation of the atom bomb. The Manhattan Project also showed that a long-
term research project could be successfully completed by a heterogeneous group
from differing backgrounds working under a single mission (O'Brien 27). This
paradigm would serve as the model for the first rehabilitation centers after
World War II.

Once World War II started, Dr. Howard A. Rusk, who had enlisted in the
Army Air Corps, was assigned to Jefferson Barracks in St. Louis, Missouri,
where he realized that patient boredom led to recidivism and a delay in soldiers
rejoining their units. By creating simple exercises of the mind and body, recidivism dropped off sharply. This moment could be called the birth of vocational
rehabilitation. As Rusk put it, "the very idea of rehabilitation medicine was derived from the notion that science, medicine, and social science should promote
democratization." Rusk saw the health of society as a result of the health of the

individual. The success of this idea led to the creation of rehabilitation centers throughout America after the war (ibid. 27-28).

After racial agitation in the summer of 1941, many black medical professionals hoped that the Army would institute reforms that would improve the status of black soldiers. Unfortunately, a "Jim Crow" segregationist mentality prevailed in the military. Hospitals maintained racially segregated wards, although eventually the Army realized that this was a waste of manpower and lifted this restriction by the end of World War II. Meanwhile, one all-black hospital was established in Tuskegee, Alabama.

The all-black staff at this hospital was led by Dr. Midian O. Bousfield, who had been the president of the National Medical Association. Bousfield was elevated to the rank of Colonel (the first black colonel in the Army medical corps) and placed in charge of the hospital at Fort Huachuca, Arizona. Many white officers doubted that any black person could be a hospital administrator, while many black doctors believed that Bousfield had abandoned their push to increase black physician participation in the military. Bousfield believed that his job performance could silence both sets of critics: "If we prove that Negro doctors can run a hospital, we will have vindicated our sponsors and perhaps contribute something to race relations, as well as the war effort" (qtd. in Hine 1290).

The assignment turned out to be a problem for Bousfield and his staff. "Apparently, there hadn't been much advance knowledge that a group of unknown Negro doctors, with relatively high rank, were descending upon [Fort Huachuca]"; the result was "some dismay on the Post." The War Department, having elevated Bousfield and his doctors, had abandoned him (ibid. 1290).

January 1945 saw a victory for the National Colored Graduate Nurses Association and its president, Mabel Staupers. Army Surgeon General Norman Kirk gave a speech in New York stating that nurses were needed. Staupers asked Kirk why, with nine thousand black nurses available, the Army had only accepted 247. Kirk made the mistake of correcting Staupers, telling her that there were only seven thousand black nurses available; with this, he also told the country that he knew the nurses were there but refused to use them. Public outcry forced Kirk to change the policy within the month, and a few days later Rear Admiral Agnew of the U.S. Navy announced that the navy medical corps would accept black nurses (ibid.).

Margaritte Gertrude Ivory-Bertram was a Lieutenant in the Army Nurse Corps, stationed at the base hospital in Fort Bragg, California. She was there when paraplegic white soldiers were brought back from Normandy:

> Forty-six young wounded white soldiers were all paralyzed from the waist down, and this was to be a short stop for them. [...] After the flight nurses brought them into the ward, the white nurse that was assigned to help me walked down the ramp, looked into the ward, turned, and walked away. [...] [She] never came back. I [...] was told the nurse didn't want to work with me because I was colored, so I worked without her. These men were paralyzed. Skin was coming off their legs and feet. I rubbed them with mineral oil, bathed them, put diapers on them, got a barber to fix their hair, and I made sure they had a good steak dinner. The soldiers didn't care what color I was. They just needed help. (Qtd. in Latty 12)

Disabled returning black soldiers "faced both sides of the two-sided coin of collective social oppression and racial discrimination" (Jefferson 1103). On the one hand, disability was stigmatized to begin with, although the Veterans Administration had developed a means-based assessment that often found black veterans to be not disabled enough to receive treatment or medical rehabilitation. In addition, being black meant that these veterans had to clear another high hurdle:

> the popular media and veterans' organizations viewed [...] disabled black ex-GIs in a derogatory light and felt that they should be grateful for *any* assistance they received. [...] [T]he findings of physicians regarding certain injuries and disease were often filtered through a socially constructed lens enveloped in gender-specific cultural and racial notions of moral depravity, physical and mental weakness, and stereotypical behavior. (Ibid. 1104)

New Yorker James C. Lee, wounded in New Guinea and hospitalized when he came home, wrote the following:

> Is this the Democracy that I've spent nearly three years defending in the Pacific? I am a disabled veteran but the deplorable conditions that exist here in this country makes me wonder if I'm going to survive as a Negro. (Qtd. in ibid. 1111)

These words were echoed by many black veterans; officially, help was available, but unofficially many whites in the armed forces remained hostile toward blacks and resentful of the medical help that was given to them. Even after President Harry Truman signed Executive Order 9981 on July 31, 1948, integrating the nation's armed forces, tensions remained between blacks and whites, both in the military and in the VA rehabilitation program.

The Black Veterans Administration was active in agitating for better treatment after World War II. However, the anti-Communist sentiment of the Cold War was also directed against advocates of civil rights,[3] and many of these protest activities were curtailed (ibid.). This was precisely the time, however, that civil rights agitation shifted to the non-violent campaign of the Southern Christian Leadership Conference and various other groups. For the next decade, a coalition of activists, young and old, black and white, put pressure on both the federal government and on local governments, especially in the Deep South. Between the Montgomery bus boycott in 1954 and the Voting Rights Act of 1965, America underwent a dramatic change in racial politics.

Just as the civil rights campaign was claiming victory over Jim Crow, the federal government was preparing to send increasing numbers of troops to Vietnam, in the first major American war since Korea. Vietnam also had the largest number of African American frontline troops, in large part because "[young white] men could avoid the draft if they were in college or well connected, but that wasn't the case for many African American men. Blacks were not well represented on draft boards. [...] Seven states had no black representation at all" (Latty 121).

The larger number of black troops brought about a larger number of black war wounded in the rehabilitation system. By this time, the G. I. Bill and vocational rehabilitation finally was forced to serve disabled black vets equitably.

In 1973, when the Nixon Administration declared "peace with honor" and began withdrawing troops from Vietnam, Congress passed the Rehabilitation Act. Specifically, one section of the bill changed rehabilitation and disabled people's reaction to it: Section 504. Disability activists used Section 504 to advance their movement's fundamental belief that attitudes obstructed disabled people, not physical or mental impairments. Section 504 helped give the movement legal ammunition to wage war on the psychoanalytic approach governing postwar vocational rehabilitation (O'Brien).

Rehabilitation policy has never been a "good fit" for soldiers leaving the Veterans Administration to re-enter civilian life. Disabled veterans, regardless of race, have problems leaving the battlefield for which they were trained as warriors, finding themselves redefined as inpatients, and later developing an outpatient regimen. This is in part due to a system that treats a "disabled veteran" as an oxymoron – a veteran, but somehow no longer connected to the military.

News articles in recent years about flagship veterans' facility Walter Reed Hospital, specifically the apparent disconnect between inpatient and outpatient treatment, shows that we still have not gotten this transition right, even in the twenty-first century. Many of the problems were noted in a ground-breaking 2007 article in the Washington *Post* by Priest and Hull. In addition to documenting the neglect and chaos caused by overcrowding a hospital opened in 1909, one documented problem is rooted in twenty-first-century technology:

> The typical soldier is required to file 22 documents with eight different commands – most of them off-post – to enter and exit the medical processing world, according to government investigators. Sixteen different information systems are used to process the forms, but few of them can communicate with one another. The Army's three personnel databases cannot read each other's files and can't interact with the separate pay system or the medical recordkeeping databases. (A01)

With the wars in Iraq and Afghanistan having gone on for five years as of this writing, the demobilization of wounded black veterans returning to America will certainly strain existing medical care and rehabilitation facilities. Complicating this is the nature of many of these troops' disabilities; the "weapon of choice" against Americans is the bomb, the mine, the rocket propelled grenade, and the suicide belt. Increasing numbers of troops are being kept alive in the field with sophisticated surgery, only to return with traumatic brain injury. As many as sixty percent of the troops have sustained some sort of traumatic brain injury (Zoroya).

This is a qualitatively different kind of injury than the rehabilitation system has ever had to deal with in large numbers. If a limb is missing or a soldier is paralyzed, the response has been to treat the body as if it were a machine that needed a spare part. There are psychological adjustment problems, but the medical system is based in part on a belief in a mind/body dichotomy. When the brain itself becomes the wounded organ, conventional wisdom and traditional treatment go out the window. The rehabilitation system in this war needs a new paradigm to help these soldiers make a transition from soldier to civilian and to help them learn to cope with their singular disability.

Today, the VA hospital system is not trouble-free, but racial discrimination seems no longer to be among its troubles.

---

[1] Slaves had no legal citizenship standing and were therefore not permitted to legally marry or have permanent families. This is not to say that there was no co-habitation resembling marriage, but "jumping the broom" was not considered a permanent mating (Patterson 189-90). In addition, some whites believed that blacks were fundamentally incapable of marriage. Brigadier General E. B. Brown of Missouri wrote that "in most Cases there are no binding marital relations which [Negroes] recognize and they have new wives and husbands with every change of the season"; as an alleged result, "small pox and venereal disease prevails to a frightening extent" among black Americans (Reid 380).

[2] This group was made up of black physicians, who were not allowed to join the American Medical Association.

[3] During the 1930s, the American Communist Party was one of the few organizations agitating for racial equality and social justice. This support from the radical Left was a mixed blessing for black Americans.

Works Cited

Bredhoff, Stacey. *American Originals*. Seattle: The U of Washington P, 2001.

Clement, Rufus E. "Problems of Demobilization and Rehabilitation of the Negro Soldier after World Wars One and Two." *Journal of Negro Education* 12.3 (1943): 533-42.

Gerber, David A. "Disabled Veterans, the State, and the Experience of Disability in Western Societies, 1914-1950." *Journal of Social History* 36.4 (2003): 899-916.

Gritzer, Glenn, and Arnold Arluke. *The Making of Rehabilitation: A Political Economy of Medical Specialization, 1890-1980*. Berkeley: U of California P, 1985.

Hickel, K. Walter. "Medicine, Bureaucracy, and Social Welfare: The Politics of Disability Compensation for American Veterans of World War I." *The New Disability History: American Perspectives*. Ed. Paul K. Longmore and Lauri Umansky. New York: New York UP, 2001. 236-67.

Hine, Darlene Clark. "Black Professionals and Race Consciousness: Origins of the Civil Rights Movement, 1890-1950." *Journal of American History* 89.4 (2006): 1-16.

Jefferson, Robert F. "'Enabled Courage': Race, Disability, and Black World War II Veterans in Postwar America." *The Historian* 65.5 (2003): 1102-24.

Latty, Yvonne. *We Were There: Voices of African American Veterans, From World War II to the War in Iraq*. New York: Amistad, 2004.

Logue, Larry M., and Peter David Blank. "'Benefit of the Doubt': African-American Civil War Veterans and Pensions." *Journal of Interdisciplinary History* 38.3 (2008): 377-99.

Mettler, Suzanne. "'The Only Good Thing Was the G.I. Bill': Effects of the Education and Training Provisions on African-American Veterans' Political Participation." *Studies in American Political Development* 19 (Spring 2005): 31-52.

Monette, Duane R., Thomas J. Sullivan, Cornell R. DeJohn. *Applied Social Research: Tool for the Human Services*. 4th ed. Fort Worth: Harcourt, Brace & Co., 1998.

O'Brien, Ruth. *Crippled Justice: The History of Modern Disability Policy in the Workplace*. Chicago: U of Chicago P, 2001.

Obermann, Carl Esco. *A History of Vocational Rehabilitation in America*. Minneapolis: T. S. Denison & Company, 1965.

Onkst, David H. "'First a Negro … Incidentally a Veteran': Black World War Two Veterans and the G. I. Bill of Rights in the Deep South, 1944-1948." *Journal of Social History* 31.3 (1998): 517-43.

Patterson, Orlando. *Slavery and Social Death: A Comparative Study*. Cambridge: Harvard UP, 1982.

Priest, Dana, and Anne Hull. "Soldiers Face Neglect, Frustration At Army's Top Medical Facility." *The Washington Post* 18 Feb. 2007. A01.

Reid, Richard. "Government Policy, Prejudice, and the Experience of Black Civil War Soldiers and Their Families." *Journal of Family History* 27.4 (2002): 374-98.

Skocpol, Theda. "America's First Social Security System: The Expansion of
    Benefits for Civil War Veterans." *Political Science Quarterly* 108.1
    (1993): 85-116.

Turner, Sarah, and John Bound. "Closing the Gap or Widening the Divide: The
    Effects of the G. I. Bill and World War II on the Educational Outcomes of
    Black Americans." *Journal of Economic History* 63.1 (2003): 145-77.

"Ward Want Vets to Unite with Tuskegee." *Pittsburgh Courier* 4 July 1925. 3.

Zoroya, Gregg. "Key Iraq Wound: Brain Trauma." *USA Today* 3 Mar. 2005.

Notes on the Contributors

Moya Bailey is a graduate candidate and scholar of critical race, feminist, and disability studies at Emory University. Her current work focuses on constructs of health and normativity within a US context. Her dissertation, "Training to Treat: A Study of Medical Education's Representation of Black Women Patients at Emory School of Medicine," explores visual and textual representation of black women in the curricular materials of the school and its subsequent impact on the lives of black women patients. She received her undergraduate degree from Spelman College where she majored in Women's Studies with a concentration in Health.

Chris Bell was Ph.D. candidate in English at Nottingham Trent University (UK) where his research examined cultural responses to the AIDS crisis. Not long before he passed away, he had begun an appointment as a post-doctoral researcher in the Center on Human Policy, Law, and Disability Studies at Syracuse University. Chris was the Modern Language Association's Delegate Assembly Representative for the Executive Committee of the Division on Disability Studies as well as a past president of the Society for Disability Studies. His essays and articles appeared, or are forthcoming, in *The Body: Readings in English and American Literature and Culture*; *Blackberries and Redbones: Critical Articulations of Black Hair/Body Politics in Africana Communities*; *Illness in the Academy: A Collection of Pathographies by Academics*; and *The Disability Studies Reader* (2nd ed.).

Stella Bolaki is a Lecturer in American Literature at the University of Glasgow. She received her Ph.D. from the University of Edinburgh in 2007 and held a postdoctoral research fellowship at the Institute for Advanced Studies in the Humanities (IASH) in 2008-09. She has also served as Co-Director of the Scottish Universities' International Summer School (SUISS), based in Edinburgh. Her research interests lie primarily in contemporary American literature and culture, with a particular focus on multi-ethnic writing. Her monograph, forthcoming by Rodopi, brings together genre and cultural theory and examines the female Bildungsroman tradition in an ethnic American and postcolonial context. She has also published articles and book chapters on such topics as cultural translation in Asian American literature, feminist transformations of fairy tales, women's short story sequences, trauma in Caribbean writing, and artists' books in the medical community. She is currently working on two projects: a monograph provisionally entitled *Poetics, Identity, and Witnessing in Contemporary Narratives of Illness and Disability* and on Audre Lorde's transatlantic relations with black diasporic communities in Europe.

Carlos Clarke Drazen is a Ph.D. candidate in Disability Studies at the University of Illinois at Chicago (UIC), with degrees in Broadcast Communications from Southern Illinois University Carbondale and Disability and Human Development from UIC. She commenced her doctoral studies in 2003. Her research examines the sociopolitical nature of disability and the use of new media to redefine that nature. Her publications include "'Ways of Seeing' in Race and Disability Research," co-authored with Glenn Fujiura, in Balcazar et al., *Race, Culture and Disability*, Jones & Bartlett, 2010; "Disability Studies as Cultural Studies," co-authored with Lennard Davis, in *Encyclopedia of Cultural Studies*, Blackwell, 2009; and "Harriet Tubman," *Encyclopedia of Disability Studies*, Sage, 2005. In 2006 she received the Edward Page-El Academic Scholarship, and the Martin Luther King, Jr. Scholarship in 2003. Currently she is Academic Coordinator for student athletes at UIC.

Cassandra Jackson is an Associate Professor of English at The College of New Jersey. Her current research and teaching interests focus on African-American literature and visual culture. Her first book, *Barriers Between Us: Interracial Sex in Nineteenth-Century American Literature*, was published by Indiana University Press in 2004. Her second book, *Violence, Visual Culture, and the Black Male Body*, was published by Routledge in 2010. She is currently working on a book entitled, *Beyond the Black Heritage Trail: Race, Place, and Public Memory in New England*, which she is co-authoring with Eve Allegra Raimon.

Michelle Jarman, Ph.D., is Assistant Professor of Disability Studies at the University of Wyoming. Her broad research interests include 20th- and 21st-century U.S. literatures, intersections between race studies, feminist theory and disability studies, and competing cultural representations of disability. Jarman's essays have appeared in journals such as *MELUS* (*Multi-Ethnic Literature of the United States*), *Review of Disability Studies*, and several literary and disability studies anthologies. Her current book project analyzes recent U.S. literary and cultural representations of cognitive, psychiatric, and other hidden disabilities to explore how "invisible" diagnoses are rendered "visible" through intersecting constructions of gender, race, and disability.

Robert McRuer is Professor of English and Deputy Chair of the Department at The George Washington University, where he teaches disability studies, queer studies, and critical theory. He is the author of *Crip Theory: Cultural Signs of Queerness and Disability* (NYU, 2006) and *The Queer Renaissance: Contemporary American Literature and the Reinvention of Lesbian and Gay Identities* (NYU, 1997). He is co-editor, with Abby L. Wilkerson, of *Desiring Disability: Queer Theory Meets Disability Studies* (Duke, 2003), which appeared as a special issue of *GLQ: A Journal of Lesbian and Gay Studies*. He is also co-editor, with Anna Mollow, of the forthcoming volume, *Sex and Disability*, which will include a new piece from Chris Bell not previously published, and hence perhaps his final publication.

Ned Mitchell is a student of queer theory and cultures living outside Washington, D.C. He graduated from the George Washington University with a B.A. in Queer Studies/Sexuality in 2008 as part of a special interdisciplinary study program. As part of this program, he studied abroad at the Universiteit van Amsterdam in 2007, focusing on gay and lesbian studies and cultural difference.

Therí Alyce Pickens received her Ph.D. in Comparative Literature from UCLA. Currently, she is a Visiting Assistant Professor at Pitzer College and also teaches at the University of Phoenix. Her current book project explores the possibilities and pitfalls of using phenomenology and disability studies as a methodological approach to Arab American and African American literature. She is also a published poet, having had her work included in *Black Renaissance Noire*.